100
Secrets
of the
Smokies

D0836007

100 Secrets of the Smokies

A Guide to the Best Undiscovered Places in the Great Smoky Mountains Area

Randall H. Duckett

AND

Maryellen Kennedy Duckett

Rutledge Hill Press®
Nashville, Tennessee

Published in Nashville, Tennessee, by Rutledge Hill Press®, 211 Seventh Avenue North, Nashville, Tennessee 37219.

Distributed in Canada by H. B. Fenn & Company, Ltd., 34 Nixon Road, Bolton, Ontario L7E 1W2.

Distributed in Australia by The Five Mile Press Pty., Ltd., 22 Summit Road, Noble Park, Victoria 3174.

Distributed in New Zealand by Tandem Press, 2 Rugby Road, Birkenhead, Auckland 10.

Distributed in the United Kingdom by Verulam Publishing, Ltd., 152a Park Street Lane, Park Street, St. Albans, Hertfordshire AL2 2AU.

Typography by E. T. Lowe Publishing Company

Library of Congress Cataloging-in-Publication Data

Duckett, Randall H., 1958–
    100 secrets of the Smokies / Randall H. Duckett and Maryellen Kennedy Duckett.
       p.   cm.
    Includes index.
    ISBN 1-55853-586-1
    1. Great Smoky Mountains Region (N.C. and Tenn.)—
Guidebooks. I. Duckett, Maryellen Kennedy, 1961–
II. Title.
F443.G7D83   1998
917.68'890453—dc21   98-5214
                                   CIP

Printed in the United States of America

3 4 5 6 7 8 9—01 00 99

To our daughters,

Katharine,
Mary,
and Cassidy,

who reveal new secrets
to us every day

Acknowledgments

Contributors: Elizabeth Duckett, Becky Johnston, Marie Hofer, and Cheryl Mitchell. Thanks for all your hard work and good humor.

We'd like to thank the following people who also helped us with the research, writing, and design of this book: Keith Bellows, David Brill, Steven Friedlander, Leasi Frye, Carolyn Gray, Kathy Hall, Mike Huddleston, David Luttrell, Tim Reid, Ken Smith, and Mary Weaver.

Thanks, too, to the many other people in East Tennessee who generously provided ideas, information, and photographs. We particularly appreciate the contributions of representatives of the Great Smoky Mountains National Park and the National Park Service.

Special thanks to Larry Stone and Mike Towle of Rutledge Hill Press.

Contents

Introduction

We got the idea for *100 Secrets of the Smokies* while stuck in traffic on Tennessee Highway 66 with our three school-age children—Katharine, Mary, and Cassidy—just off Interstate 40 in East Tennessee. We were there because we had promised the kids that we would take them to Dollywood, the Pigeon Forge amusement park owned by Smoky Mountains native Dolly Parton.

While sitting there we couldn't help but notice one of the most spectacularly beautiful sights in America, off in the distance under a striking blue sky: the Great Smoky Mountains. That moment became the basis of our mutual inspiration to learn more about the Smokies and the surrounding area. Our search since then has unveiled dozens of secrets now packaged here in what we believe is an indispensable guide for traveling the back roads of this part of Appalachia. The idea is twofold: to avoid the bad traffic altogether and to discover its best treasures.

More than five hundred thousand acres at the southern tip of the Appalachian Mountains were set aside in the 1930s as a preserve for countless plants and animals, left in a natural state not all that different from when the mountains were formed 250 million years ago. Millennia later, the Cherokee, the mountains' first residents, called the area "the place of blue smoke" for the misty haze that often hovers over the peaks; and the name—the Smokies—stuck.

It's said that you can find every kind of flora that grows between Georgia and Maine within the park's boundaries. Who are we to argue? The wilderness is home to an amazing diversity of wildlife, from organisms too small for the naked eye to four-hundred-pound black bears. Miles of cool clear rivers, streams, and waterfalls rush and gush through the mountains. And ridge after ridge of two-thousand-foot-high peaks seem to stretch on forever. Such natural splendor makes the Great Smoky Mountains National Park a haven for overnight campers, serious backpackers, day hikers, picnickers, sightseers, and anyone else wanting to escape the stress of modern life.

A host of other attractions surround the park, which sits on the Tennessee–North Carolina border: water parks, outlet malls, go-cart tracks, miniature golf courses, car museums, souvenir shops, music theaters, bed-and-breakfasts, pancake houses, high-rise hotels, one-story motels, and much, much more. Pigeon Forge and Gatlinburg, on the Tennessee side, and Cherokee, on the North Carolina side, are the major gateways to the mountains, with wonderful things to do and see everywhere within an hour or so's drive from the heart of the park. The combination of natural and man-made attractions makes the mountains one of the most popular vacation destinations in America; the area hosts about ten million visitors a year.

The downside of the Smokies' popularity is the severe crowding. A veritable parking lot of cars, pickup trucks, vans, and campers can often be seen stretched along the main route from the interstate through Sevierville, Pigeon Forge, and Gatlinburg. The contrast between the unspoiled beauty of the peaks in the distance and the spoiled eyesore of the miles of vehicles is striking. As we sat there inhaling fumes that day, we started to feel sorry for the people trapped in the cars around us. True, we were also trapped, but we knew it would probably be the last time for us.

We've lived near the Smokies for more than fifteen years, which has given us ample opportunity to experience what the mountains are all about. Folks who spend much of their vacations stuck on the main roads miss out on a lot of the area's natural splendor, rich history, fascinating culture, and, perhaps most importantly, contact with the friendly people that make East Tennessee and western North Carolina so special.

We turned off Tennessee Highway 66 at the junction with U.S. Highway 411/441 and within a few moments were free of the crush of cars and taking the traffic-free back way to a day at Dollywood (see Secret 64). Along the way we encountered nary a tourist and avoided the tangle of vehicles that was still inching its way somewhere behind us. We were on to something.

Despite the millions of visitors and the unrestrained development along the main tourist routes, the Smokies and surrounding area still feature great getaway destinations and the convenient means to get to those places—if you know where to find them. With this book, you soon will.

As we pulled into the back entrance to Dollywood, we decided it would be a worthy endeavor to tell folks otherwise gridlocked in traffic about the best lesser-known, off-the-beaten-track, undiscovered places and things to do in our home area. The result is this book, a collection of one hundred ways to get the most out of your vacation in the Smokies. Unlike other travel guides, it doesn't lump the Smokies with other parts of Tennessee. Rather, it's based on the premise that you've come or are coming here to stay awhile, and you want ideas for things to do and see in proximity to the Great Smoky Mountains National Park. We've come up with a wide variety of activities that will appeal to almost anyone—from those who love a challenging hike in the woods to those whose idea of adventure is shopping for the perfect quilt.

How did we choose which secrets to include? We'd like to say we followed a scientific process that factored in location, cost, quality, appeal to adults and kids, and a mixture of things visitors might want to do. We did some of that, but in the end it came down to simply choosing those things we would recommend to visiting out-of-town relatives (ones we like). We would do all we could to steer them toward special experiences and away from traffic jams and tourist traps—and that's just what we've done for you.

Okay, so none of the book's suggestions are totally *secret*. It depends on your perspective. Perhaps you will discover a great experience for the first time or learn something new and interesting that helps you squeeze more out of your stay in the Smokies. Remember, something old hat to one person could be a revelation to another. That's what this book is all about: revealing secrets to you.

To help you better navigate *100 Secrets of the Smokies,* we've designated each suggestion as falling into one of the following six categories:

- Places to eat
- Places to stay
- Adventures
- Attractions
- Getting around
- FYI

Each secret is identified with an icon for its category so that you can easily find the perfect place to take a hike or have dinner. Under the heading Secret Information for each item, we give the appropriate details about the secret (location, address, phone, hours, and so on).

For each secret, we've also included a Top Secret, an extra bit of inside information that will help you get even more out of the recommended place or activity.

Every effort has been made to verify all information as being accurate at the time of publication, but we offer no guarantees. Also, the inclusion of a place or activity in this book does not construe a guarantee or responsibility on our part to the entry's products, services, or safety. And, of course, always be careful when exploring the Great Smoky Mountains National Park or other wilderness areas. Obey the rules, respect nature, and use caution and common sense.

We hope you enjoy the book and that it helps you have a more fun and memorable vacation in the Smokies. Please send along any other secrets you discover. We'll pay fifty dollars per item if one or more of your ideas are used in a future edition of *100 Secrets of the Smokies* (see page 257 for details).

—RANDALL H. DUCKETT AND MARYELLEN KENNEDY DUCKETT

To help you better navigate *100 Secrets of the Smokies*, we've organized our suggestions into the following categories (the icons identify into which category each secret falls). See the maps on the following pages to find out in which part of the Smokies the secrets are located.

 PLACES TO EAT—great spots for everything from a quick snack to a gourmet dinner.

 PLACES TO STAY—best places to find not only a bed (or a campsite) but also to have a special experience.

 ADVENTURES—outdoor recreation and other activities that answer the age-old vacation question, "What do you want to do today?"

 ATTRACTIONS—sights, shops, and amusements that answer the next question, "I dunno, what do you want to do?"

 GETTING AROUND—roads to take to avoid the tourist traffic and to get you where you really want to be—having fun.

 FYI—bits of background on the Smokies and other information to help you get more out of your visit to the mountains.

Complete Map of Smokies Area

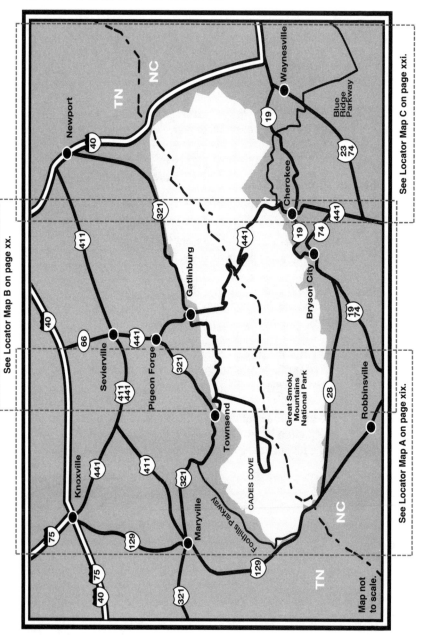

Locator Map A
(western Smokies)

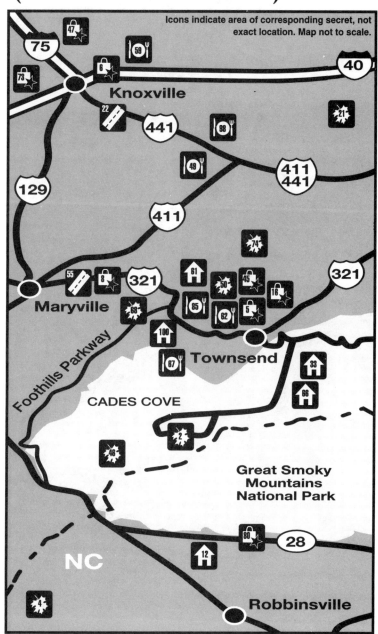

Icons indicate area of corresponding secret, not exact location. Map not to scale.

Knoxville

Maryville

Townsend

CADES COVE

Foothills Parkway

Great Smoky
Mountains
National Park

NC

Robbinsville

Locator Map B
(central Smokies)

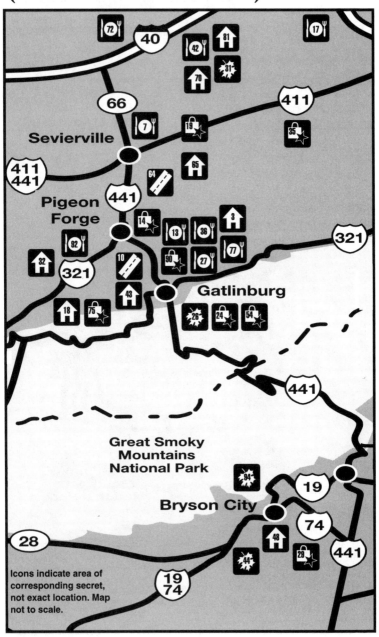

Locator Map C
(eastern Smokies)

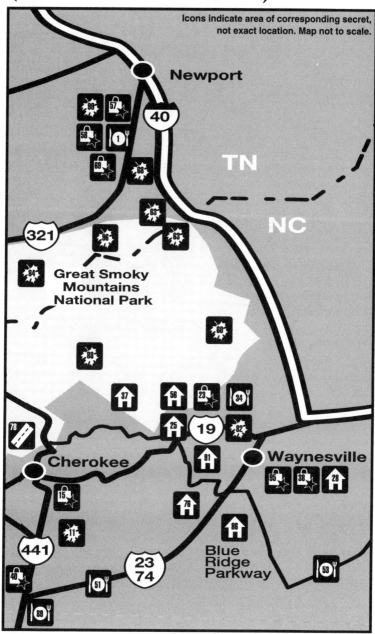

Icons indicate area of corresponding secret, not exact location. Map not to scale.

Newport

TN

NC

321

Great Smoky
Mountains
National Park

Cherokee

Waynesville

Blue
Ridge
Parkway

100
Secrets
of the
Smokies

The Front Porch Restaurant

Tijuana in Tennessee

Aline Guzman spent twenty years as a housewife raising her seven children in Pontiac, Michigan. Between cooking, cleaning, and car pooling she would occasionally head south to visit her sister, who had settled in the foothills of the Smokies. Guzman fell in love with the mountains, and she and her husband, Louis, who designed auto parts, bought some land and made plans to move. "We kept putting it off," she recalls, "so one day I told him, 'Next year I'm leaving for Tennessee with or without you.'"

Louis stayed put and Aline kept her promise. She packed up her youngest four children and headed to Cosby, Tennessee, in the shadow of the Smokies. Scared at first to be on her own, she quickly made a good home for her family. After awhile she got bored and decided that she wanted to work. "Having spent all my time raising kids, the only thing I knew how to do was cook," Guzman recalls. She had learned how to make Mexican food from her mother-in-law, a native of America's neighbor to the south, and feeding a family of nine over the years had taught her a thing or two about creating nutritious meals for large groups.

Guzman put her knowledge and experience to good use. She found an old cement and wood slab building and, with two thousand dollars, opened what she calls "the world's only Mexican-bluegrass restaurant."

"I thought about calling it something like La Hacienda," she says, "but a couple of people around here said, 'What's that? Chinese?' So I named it the Front Porch, because I wanted to create the atmosphere of a southern front porch where you can kick back, listen to music, and watch life go by." The early days were lean, but the restaurant eventually started to attract an eclectic mix of local mountain people, hippies, and members of wealthy families who had founded Gatlinburg and Pigeon Forge.

Pale blue and pink and dotted with plants, the Front Porch looks like it belongs on a Tijuana roadside.

The Front Porch still offers a funky, laid-back atmosphere and authentic Mexican cuisine made from scratch. The pale blue and pink, plant-dotted building looks like it belongs on a Tijuana roadside, not in Tennessee. Inside it's a casual mix of Mexican trinkets, many of which have been brought back by Aline and Louis from their annual treks south of the border. Huge sombreros (which our daughters love trying on) are scattered about. The walls are adorned with photos of Louis's family, including his grandfather and grandmother, rich landowners who fled Mexico during the revolution. His grandfather, the story goes, was spared death at Pancho Villa's hand when his grandmother lined up their children in front of him and told the revolutionary that if he wanted to kill Louis's ancestor, Villa would have to kill the whole family.

The Front Porch is not Taco Bell. Guzman makes everything fresh, from huevos rancheros (fried eggs over tortilla chips slathered in spicy sauce) to cadillo, a sort of Mexican beef stew. Bowing to more American tastes, the menu also features beef ribs, spaghetti, and hamburgers. Vegetarians can opt for the portabella mushroom, which is seasoned, grilled whole, and served with jasmine rice and black beans; it didn't make the latest menu revision, but just ask and Guzman will be happy to make it for you.

The Front Porch is open only on Friday, Saturday, and Sunday. At about eight or so each evening the music starts. Guzman calls these "hoot 'n' holler" nights. Cocke County is dry, so customers must bring their own beer, sometimes in coolers. Then it's time to kick back and stomp your feet to the music of groups like Two Shades of Blue, which plays both bluegrass and blues. Sunday is open microphone night; so, if you've got the urge to be the next Garth or Reba, feel free to take the stage. The place never gets too rowdy for kids, who will have a great time dancing in front of the stage as the band picks country tunes.

Louis finally retired in the mideighties and joined Aline in Tennessee. The two are celebrating their fiftieth anniversary in 1998. Count on a huge party.

Secret Information

Location: On U.S. Highway 321, between I-40 (exit 435) and Cosby, Tennessee.
Address: Highway 321, Cosby, Tennessee 37722.
Phone: (423) 487-2875.
Hours: Noon to 10:00 P.M., Friday through Sunday.
Prices: Entrees range from $4.95 to $9.95.
Credit cards: None.
Details: Customers are welcome to come, hang out, and listen to music all night, but they're asked to spend at least $5 per person for a meal.

TOP SECRET

The other must-see spot in Cosby, just a stone's throw from the Front Porch, is Fort Marx, so named for its eighty-something-year-old owner Fred Marx. Unfortunately, we can't recommend it because it sells what Granny from *The Beverly Hillbillies* called her "rumatiz medicine" and other homemade libations, which are illegal, strictly speaking. We'd tell you to ask the folks at the restaurant to give you directions to where only adults can imbibe mountain margaritas before dinner, but it would be wrong, wrong, wrong.

Peddle Power

2

On Saturday mornings we like to get the kids up early, pile into the van, and head to the mountains to visit Cades Cove. It's one of the most popular areas of the park, drawing two million visitors a year to gawk at the five-thousand-acre valley in the western part of the Great Smoky Mountains National Park.

A single-lane, one-way, eleven-mile road circles the cove, making it one of the area's most popular auto tours. It is also the starting point for some of the park's best trails, including the hugely popular and often overcrowded route to Abrams Falls. There are several nineteenth-century homesteads where history lovers can stop and wander through; and park rangers frequently lead tours of such areas as Cable Mill, a gristmill constructed in 1868. Also, the cove is a good place to spot white-tailed deer, black bear, and other wildlife, particularly in the early morning or late afternoon.

At the height of tourist season, the road is one steady stream of exhaust-belching vehicles. That's why we like to go on Saturday mornings, when the loop road is closed until 10:00 A.M. And there's the secret. We pull into a parking place, unload our bikes, and peddle past the long row of tourists waiting for the road to reopen later in the day. We spend the next couple of hours cycling around the cove road, enjoying the engineless sights and sounds. Without all the vehicular traffic it's easy to imagine what it must have been like for early settlers to make their homes in a cove cut off from the rest of civilization.

The eleven-mile road is a little hilly but doesn't have any long climbs. At worst, you might have to hop off your bike for a few minutes and walk it up a hill. Be careful as you head down some of the slopes, however. You can pick up speed pretty quickly and encounter unexpected turns. Several bikers are injured each year, so wear a helmet.

The cove has been closed to motorized traffic on Saturday morning for years, but only since 1995 have Wednesday mornings been added. Fewer people know about the midweek closing; and if you want to tour the cove when it's even more deserted, that's the day to go. Our family always feels recharged after such an outing, and we think riding a bike is the only way to see Cades Cove.

Secret Information

Location: At the end of Laurel Creek Falls Road in the western end of the Great Smoky Mountains National Park.

Hours: The Cades Cove Loop Road is closed to motorized vehicles from 7:00 A.M. to 10:00 A.M. on Wednesday and Saturday.

Prices: Bikes can be rented at the Cades Cove campground for $3.25 an hour starting at 7:00 A.M. on the days the loop road is closed to traffic and at 9:00 A.M. the rest of the week. Call (423) 448-9034 for more information.

Details: If you don't want to ride the entire loop, you can trim the ride down by seven miles by cutting across the cove on Sparks Lane, or by three miles by taking Hyatt Road.

TOP SECRET

If you don't want to see Cades Cove under peddle power, the best way to tour it is on a park-ranger-led hayride. Trips around the loop leave from the road's entrance at 7:00 in the morning and 7:00 at night (except on Wednesday and Saturday, when the morning trek leaves at 10:00) from June through August. The schedule changes slightly during the fall foliage season. The cost is $7 per person. Call (423) 448-6286 for more information.

Picture Perfect

Here's a story straight from a Harlequin romance: Lisa Hippensteal's parents ran Mountain View Inn (built in 1916) in Gatlinburg, Tennessee, for more than forty years before it was demolished to make way for an amusement park in the early nineties. Around the same time, Lisa married Vern Hippensteal, a successful painter, in fourteen-degree weather on the summit of Mount LeConte, the highest peak in the Great Smoky Mountains. As a wedding present, he vowed to reproduce the Appalachian retreat in which she grew up, on a fifteen-acre tract just north of the national park. It's no wonder that Hippensteal's Mountain View Inn is one of the most beautiful and romantic bed-and-breakfasts in the Smokies.

The three-story, stone and wood main building boasts the same wraparound porches as the original inn. Guests sit in rocking chairs or on porch swings and savor views of Greenbrier Pinnacle, Mount LeConte, and Mount Harrison. The interior decor is a work of art. Vern, who has two galleries elsewhere in Gatlinburg, paints intricate watercolors of his beloved Smokies—sunsets and snow-covered landscapes, wildlife and waterfalls, fawns and flowers. His and Lisa's artistic touches are evident everywhere. The floor of the huge lobby, for instance, is an offset checkerboard of black-and-white tile. The dining room is all green and white with tables elegantly set for two, as couples are the most frequent guests. Hundreds of prints of Vern's paintings cover almost every inch of the inn's walls. (Like one? Buy it. The prints are all for sale.)

There are only nine bedrooms in the main building. A recently completed and smaller second building has two more guest rooms upstairs. Lisa's parents, Jane and Tom Woods, Mountain View's original managers, live on the first floor. Bedrooms in both buildings feature French doors that open onto the porches with views of the mountains. (To avoid the prying eyes of other guests, close the curtains.) All have gas fireplaces and large bathrooms with whirlpools just right for two.

This is a picture-perfect spot for a romantic getaway, whether it be a honeymoon or a retreat to rekindle a long relationship. Thanks, Vern, for giving a present from the past not only to your bride, Lisa, but to the rest of us.

Secret Information

Location: Off Birds Creek Road, just north of the Great Smoky Arts and Crafts Community loop, east of downtown Gatlinburg.

Address: P.O. Box 707, Gatlinburg, Tennessee 37738.

Phone: (800) 527-8110 or (423) 436-5761.

Rates: $95–$125 for two; includes breakfast and evening baked snacks; for a stay of seven days, the seventh night is free.

Season: Year-round.

Credit cards: American Express, Discover, MasterCard, Visa.

Details: Everything in the inn is designed to cater to couples; the inn isn't really right for families, although children aren't turned away. Holidays and fall foliage season might be booked up to a year in advance.

TOP SECRET

Look carefully at Vern Hippensteal's paintings on display at Hippensteal's Mountain View Inn and you'll find little fairy figures tucked inside a leaf, curled up behind a plant, or peeking over a log. Hidden in some of them are words or phrases like "Love" and "I love Lisa." The fairies supposedly represent his two children—all the figures were female until his son was born. Guests have been so fascinated with the fairies that some have sent Vern fairy figurines, a collection of which are on display at the inn's office.

A Marriage Made in Heaven

An October 1996 wedding between two roads, two national forests, and two communities took place high in the mountains along the Tennessee–North Carolina border. Six hundred people attended the ceremony to dedicate one of the nation's newest scenic roads—the Cherohala Skyway. The spectacular fifty-one-mile stretch between Tellico Plains, Tennessee, and Robbinsville, North Carolina, just south of the Smokies, isn't even labeled the Cherohala Skyway on most maps; but it has quickly become known as a piece of pavement that rivals the best sections of the granddaddy of scenic roads, the Blue Ridge Parkway.

Cherohala is a combination of the names of the two national forests south of the Smokies that the road spans—the Cherokee National Forest in Tennessee and the Nantahala National Forest in North Carolina. It skims the sky at up to 5,472 feet past fields of wildflowers, Catawba rhododendrons, and mountain laurels; and it offers views of the Joyce Kilmer Memorial Forest-Slickrock Wilderness, the waters of Santeetlah Lake, and countless rolling ridges of virgin forest. Along the way there's a swimming beach, campsites, bike trails, fishing at Indian Boundary, hiking trails, and wildlife-viewing areas.

To locals, the beauty of the road is more utilitarian. The idea for the skyway started back in the late fifties when the TV show *Wagon Train* was popular. Some Tellico Plains Kiwanis Club members joked that the local roads connecting them to North Carolina were so bad that they should organize a wagon train of their own. The offhand remark turned into a way to publicize and raise funds for the proposed new road. In June 1958 the community organized a wagon train that left Tellico Plains for Murphy, North Carolina, and included 67 old-fashioned wagons and 325 equestrians. Construction on the skyway started in 1965 and the wagon-train tradition continued every year (except 1990), reaching up to 117 wagons and 400 horseback riders, until the road was nearly completed. The last wagons rolled on July 4, 1996.

Modern-day travel between Tellico Plains and Robbinsville is much easier, but for vacationers the point isn't the destination, it's the journey that counts. It takes you along a new and largely undiscovered route that already holds the distinction of being one of only twenty U.S. highways designated by the Federal Highway Administration as National Scenic Byways.

Secret Information

Location: The Cherohala Skyway is clearly marked starting at Tellico Plains and Robbinsville. To find it on a map, look for Tennessee Highway 165 in Tennessee and North Carolina Highway 143 in North Carolina.

Details: The drive takes about two hours if you allow some time to stop and savor the views. For more information, write or call the Cheoah Ranger District in North Carolina, U.S. Forest Service, Route 1, Box 16A, Robbinsville, North Carolina 28771, (704) 479-6431, or the Tellico Ranger District in Tennessee, U.S. Forest Service, Tellico Plains, Tennessee 37385, (423) 253-2520.

TOP SECRET

Be sure to stop at the Unicoi Crest Overlook, where three states can be viewed from one spot. Tennessee is westward, North Carolina is eastward, and Georgia is to the southwest. The dedication of the Tennessee and North Carolina highways and national forests also took place here, with more than six hundred onlookers.

5 Hands-on Learning

When Beryl Lumpkin was a little girl she would gather together her friends and teach them tricks she had learned during summers and weekends at her grandparents' home in the country. She would show the other boys and girls how to make "grasshopper nests" (tiny baskets) out of English plantain or how to paint with the juice of poke berries—just two of the skills her family had used in daily life since they first moved to upper East Tennessee in the 1800s.

"I've been an artist all my life," Lumpkin says, "but I guess I've always been a teacher, too."

Lumpkin later spent twenty years painting, basket weaving, and managing arts organizations, but she always dreamed of opening a school where "I could perpetuate our mountain heritage and keep people aware of the skills that our ancestors developed for enjoyment and daily living. In those days there were no stores and you made whatever you needed by hand—toys, furniture, baskets, quilts, tools."

Lumpkin's dream became a reality when she opened the Earthtide School of Folk Arts in Townsend, Tennessee. The renovated two-story garage filled with studios is the perfect place to go if you want to spend anywhere from two hours to a few weeks indulging your creativity. You can learn authentic Appalachian arts such as spinning, weaving, basketry, pottery, painting, sculpture, woodworking, drawing, stained-glass making, and furniture making from some of the Smoky Mountains' most accomplished artisans. During the weekend weaving course, taught by local working textile makers, classes of about six students are taught to "wind a warp," which means to measure yarn in a certain way. They create a textile design, put yarn on a loom, and produce a small piece of work such as a scarf or table runner to take home. Shorter workshops teach skills like stained-glass making and gourd painting. For some basketry classes, students ven-

Some of the Smoky Mountains' most accomplished artisans can be seen at Earthtide working on authentic Appalachian works of art.

ture into the woods to gather kudzu and other vines to weave into works of art. The lineup of classes is ever changing and frequently tied to the season.

For those who don't want to make their own art but want to take home something beautiful, Lumpkin has opened the Earthtide Gallery in a building next to the school's studios. The gallery features both traditional and contemporary pieces, including handmade quilts, furniture, tapestries, sculptures, and blown glass, for two dollars to four thousand dollars. "We have the work of some people who are second- and third-generation weavers from Gatlinburg," Lumpkin adds. "Their creations are real treasures."

Lumpkin admits that she's not making money from the school or the gallery and that she supplements her income by teaching art at local schools. But she's sticking with Earthtide because creating art and teaching others to do it are personal passions. "What drives me is the belief that all of contemporary design and art is based on traditional skills," she says. "People have got to learn the basics to expand their creativity, and the basics came from the cultures that settled in these mountains."

Secret Information

Location: U.S. Highway 321, in Townsend, Tennessee.

Address: 7645 Lamar Alexander Parkway, Townsend, Tennessee 37882.

Phone: (423) 448-1106.

Hours: Gallery open 10:00 A.M. to 5:00 P.M., Tuesday through Saturday, from March 1 through December 20. Classes are offered during every month except January.

Prices: Classes cost about $10 an hour.

Credit cards: Discover, MasterCard, Visa.

Details: Lumpkin suggests calling her before your vacation to ask about upcoming classes, although vacationers are welcome to drop in and sign up for whatever workshops are being offered, if there's space.

TOP SECRET

Earthtide School of Folk Arts proprietor Beryl Lumpkin is also a naturalist who has written books on plant life in the Smokies. A couple times a year she leads wild-edibles classes into the woods, where she guides students in gathering leaves, flowers, roots, and other vegetation. Then the group cooks a gourmet meal using the foods they've found in the forest. Meals include quiche made with wild greens and herbs, dandelion muffins, and staghorn sumac tea.

Knoxville Zoo

Wildlife Watching

Bears, deer, and other wild animals live in the Smokies, and chances are you'll glimpse a few as you hike or drive through the national park. The only way to guarantee an up-close-and-personal encounter with these animals and hundreds of other more exotic beasts, though, is to take a short drive a few miles west on Interstate 40 for a day at the Knoxville Zoo.

Knoxville, Tennessee isn't a big city, but it boasts a big-time zoological park. Bordered by the interstate and an urban neighborhood, the 130-acre zoo is a leafy oasis filled with winding tree-lined paths, Plexiglas-enclosed natural habitats, and an assortment of more than one thousand animals. Gorilla Valley, for example, is a state-of-the-art indoor/outdoor natural habitat for the two resident silverback males. The North American River Otter exhibit has earned awards for its design, and Pridelands, home to the majestic big cats, is *The Lion King* come to life. Over in the Kid's Zoo, baby goats, lambs, and llamas make friends with kids of the two-legged variety. There is also a tropical walk-through aviary called Birds of Central America. The latest addition, Chimpanzee Ridge, is scheduled to open in 1998.

The summer brings with it a laundry list of special events and attractions. That's when the zoo regularly hosts exotic visitors to attract out-of-towners: Recent years have featured everything from warthogs to white alligators. The Bird Show, held under the trees at an outdoor amphitheater, is a warm-weather exhibition of hawks and other high flyers that is not to be missed; and the Ice Cream Weekend held in Safari Glen is a cool way to spend a hot July day.

Set aside the better part of a day to get the most out of a zoo tour. "This is not a place where the animals are behind bars and you just race through and check off each one you see as you pass by," zoo spokesperson Nancy Young says. "There are more natural habitats

Camel rides for children add to the fun at the Knoxville Zoo. (Photo by Jane Burke Taylor)

here, and that requires visitors to come and sit and watch over a period of time to truly appreciate the animals and observe them."

Our favorite thing to do is to observe the animals as they participate in the zoo's model enrichment program, which is designed to reproduce activities the animals would do in their own natural habitat. Friday, for instance, is bone day. The zookeepers throw bones (usually cow or horse) to the big cats, which use them as chew toys. On other days the staff might give the gorillas phone books to tear apart or hand the baboons paper towel holders filled with peanut butter for them to play with. One year a farmer donated two-hundred-plus pumpkins to the zoo, so the keepers put them in with the elephants to see what they would do. The elephants walked around, picked them up, then finally one giant walked over and stepped on one and started a spontaneous smashing-pumpkins event.

Secret Information

Location: Just off I-40 (exit 392), in Knoxville, Tennessee.

Address: P.O. Box 6040, Knoxville, Tennessee 37914.

Phone: (423) 637-5331.

Hours: 9:30 A.M. to 6:00 P.M., every day except Christmas.

Prices: $6.95 for adults; $3.95 for children, ages 3 to 12, and seniors; free for kids, age 2 and under. Parking: $2.

Credit cards: American Express, Discover, MasterCard, Visa.

Details: Call ahead to find out what animal enrichment events and other programs are scheduled for the week.

TOP SECRET

The Knoxville Zoo's Saturday morning Breakfast with the Beasts program lets you park at a secret back entrance to the zoo before the gates open and slip into the Tiger Tops Cafe at 8:30 A.M. for a light Continental breakfast. Then a guide takes you through the empty (no humans) zoo to visit the living quarters of the giraffes, gorillas, and other animals—an extremely cool experience for school-age kids. Once the program concludes at 10:00 A.M., you're free to roam the zoo with everyone else. The price, which includes zoo admission and parking for the remainder of the day, is $15 for adults, $10 for kids over 2, and free for kids 2 and under. Call a few months in advance of your Smokies vacation to make reservations.

7

Blast from the Past

Locals call eateries like Virgil's '50s Restaurant "meat and threes," for their blue plate specials featuring a meat such as fried chicken, chicken-fried steak, country ham, or barbecued ribs, and your choice of three vegetables such as mashed potatoes, creamed corn, green beans, and fried okra. Such places hearken back to an era in the South when food was all fried, smothered in gravy, and served with heaping helpings of grease-soaked side dishes. Virgil's, however, combines this country flavor with a fifties theme. Both Elvis the country boy and Elvis the King of rock 'n' roll would have felt at home there.

Virgil's is billed as "Sevierville's oldest continually operating cafe." That's true, sort of. Since 1929 there has always been a cafe at 109 East Bruce Street in Sevierville, Tennessee. But it hasn't always been the same restaurant or run by the same people. In 1989, Virgil Carr and his mom, Mary, took over the spot and developed the fifties theme based on their own love of the decade. They redecorated with turquoise and peach booths, black-topped tables, and a black-and-white tiled floor, accented by pink neon lights and mobiles made from pink plastic hula hoops with .45 records strung from them. Classic tunes like "Earth Angel," "Ain't That a Shame," and "Goin' to the Chapel" play softly over the speakers. The ice cream is hand dipped from a frosty glass-topped freezer, and the thick shakes are churned in shiny metal canisters at an old-fashioned soda fountain. There are life-size cutouts of Betty Boop and James Dean, and an entire wall of the back dining room is covered with *Life* magazine pictures of fifties cars and stars like Marilyn Monroe, Elvis, and, of course, Sevierville's favorite daughter, Dolly Parton, whose relatives have dined a time or two at Virgil's.

A picture of Mary Carr is on the Home Cooked Meals section of the restaurant's menu. Most days you can sneak a peek in the kitchen: She takes pride in serving Virgil's customers only "country cooked" vegetables like pintos, fried okra, black-eyed peas, and pickled beets. With other truly southern restaurants, Mary cooks up "vegetables" that would be booted into another food group north of the Mason-Dixon line. Take your pick from among deviled eggs, baked apples, and corn-bread dressing and gravy. The menu also features catfish and all-day breakfast favorites such as the Big Bopper, which includes three eggs cooked to order, a meat, hash browns or grits, and, of course, a bowl of gravy with homemade biscuits. Mary also is well loved for her homemade cream pies.

Secret Information

Location: Just off the town square, in Sevierville, Tennessee.
Address: 109 East Bruce Street, Sevierville, Tennessee 37876.
Hours: 8:00 A.M. until 3:00 P.M. (9:00 P.M. on Friday night).
Prices: From $2.25 for a bowl of homemade chili with corn bread to $12.95 for a ten-ounce rib eye with two sides and dinner bread.
Credit cards: MasterCard, Visa.
Details: Dress is casual and there's a children's menu. In addition to breakfast and traditional country items, there are salads, burgers, and sandwiches.

TOP SECRET

Virgil's '50s Restaurant doubles as the Sevierville bus station, just as every cafe before it at this location has done since the thirties. During World War II local boys would enjoy a last sandwich and shake with their friends and family inside the restaurant before boarding buses bound for Knoxville and on to basic training. Today customers can sip coffee inside or sit on the park bench outside Virgil's front window to wait for the daily bus to nearby Pigeon Forge and Gatlinburg.

8

What Am I Bid?

Every Friday night at about 6:45 folks start arriving for the weekly bidding at Hall's Furniture and Auction just outside Maryville, Tennessee. Inside the disheveled, white-frame structure, Ronnie and Sheila Hall busily give out bidding numbers and get ready to try to sell a fraction of the stuff that fills every nook and cranny of the building. Some might call the eclectic collection of furniture, pictures, clocks (none set correctly), light fixtures, vinyl records, linens, guns, perfume bottles, toys, and even, we imagine, the kitchen sink, *junk*. Others might more kindly think of it as kitsch, collectibles, or valuable antiques. As Bruno, the Halls' pet chihuahua, supervises, Ronnie begins the bidding precisely at seven o'clock. He does the best he can to move merchandise to the one hundred or so locals who usually show up for some Smokies-style Friday night entertainment.

Ronnie and Sheila are masters of stimulating the crowd. One of their methods for building audience interest is by chatting up the history behind each item. They're also good at putting on a show. Bidding will be slow on an item like a 1957 high school annual from out of state, when Ron will turn to Sheila and, acting as if no one else is in the room, tell her that he recognized a picture of an old girlfriend of his. She'll give him a disapproving smirk and suddenly the bidding will pick up and the old yearbook will be sold. *Regis and Kathy Lee* come to mind.

The Halls pick which items to sell. Offerings include such treasures (at least to some) as a Barney Rubble cookie jar, Patti Page or Perry Como albums (from which Ronnie likes to sing a few lines), antique jewelry, and stuff even the Halls can't identify. Ronnie keeps things moving at a fast pace, although he sometimes misses a bid, explaining, "I've only got one good eye. The other's a fake." The auction usually ends in the wee hours of the morning.

Secret Information

Location: U.S. Highway 321, just east of Maryville, Tennessee.
Address: 3501 East Lamar Alexander Parkway, Maryville, Tennessee 37804.
Phone: (423) 983-1598.
Hours: Auction at 7:00 P.M. every Friday night year-round; the antique store is also open, Monday through Thursday, 11:00 A.M. to 5:00 P.M., and Friday, from 11:00 A.M. until the auction ends.
Credit cards: MasterCard, Visa (5 percent surcharge for using a credit card).

TOP SECRET

Hall's Furniture and Auction is only one of the hundreds of places in the Smoky Mountains area conducive to hunting for antiques, collectibles, or just plain junk. Another of our favorite spots is the Esau's Antiques and Collectibles Show held the third weekend of every month at Chilhowee Park just off Interstate 40 (exit 392) in Knoxville. About three hundred dealers hawk everything from British antiques to Barbies. April and October are "extravaganza months" at the show and draw double the normal number of dealers. Admission is $3 ($2 for senior citizens); $4 in April and October, and the show's hours are 9:00 A.M. to 5:30 P.M., Saturday and Sunday. On Friday serious shoppers can pay to get into the building where the show is held, while dealers are setting up, so as to get first crack at all the stuff. Call (800) 588-ESAU or (423) 588-1233 for more information.

9

Birth of a
National Park

It was in the 1920s and Ann Davis, the daughter of a prominent Kentucky family, and her husband, Willis, then the president of Knoxville Iron Works, were out in Yellowstone National Park seeing the sights. Turning to her spouse, Ann asked, "Why can't we have a national park in the Great Smokies?" That simple question and the couple's ensuing success in drumming up enthusiasm among their influential friends back home eventually led to the founding, in 1934, of the Great Smoky Mountains National Park.

The process wasn't easy—in fact, previous attempts had failed. Although eighteen other national parks had already been established by 1924, they were created out of lands already held by the federal government. The Smokies, however, were entirely in private hands. The vast majority of the land belonged to logging and pulpwood companies, with the rest spread among some twelve hundred farms and more than five thousand tiny plots. In 1925, Ann Davis became a representative to the Tennessee legislature and introduced the bill that eventually led to the acquisition of the seventy-five-thousand-acre Little River Lumber Company tract. That area would become the heart of the park's acquisitions.

It took more than a decade to raise the estimated ten million dollars necessary for purchase, then to survey, appraise, and acquire the land. There were plenty of problems, not the least of which was that landowners, on hearing the spiel to Congress and potential donors about the magnificence of the landscape, wanted to hold out for more money. There were triumphs, too, such as when John D. Rockefeller Jr. contributed five million dollars to help. In 1934, 515,226 acres officially became the Great Smoky Mountains National Park.

This effort to preserve nature resulted in the displacement of the more than seven thousand people residing on park lands. Cades

President Franklin D. Roosevelt helped dedicate the Great Smoky Mountains National Park at its 1934 opening. (Great Smoky Mountains National Park photo)

Cove, for example, was home to about six or seven hundred people; there were a schoolhouse, three churches, and a gristmill. Most of the residents of that community were forced to leave Cades Cove in the thirties and forties. Much later to leave were the part-time residents of Elkmont, who had formed the Appalachian Club in 1907 and had built a hotel-clubhouse and log cabins. The quarters became the vacation and summer retreat for a virtual Who's Who of area residents, principally Knoxvillians. Many of the original Elkmonters did much to help establish the national park. Name, rank, and longevity on-site, plus agreements forged with the Department of the Interior, helped them stay longer than other residents on park land. Most members of the Elkmont community had left by the early 1990s.

Back in the twenties, long before there were sprawling cities and countrysides laced with superhighways, it was tough for Ann Davis and the many other champions of the park to sell the idea of setting aside such a large chunk of wilderness for future generations. As you climb to the top of Mount LeConte, tour Cades Cove, or camp out at Elkmont, say a silent thank-you that the Davises succeeded.

Secret Information

To learn more about the history of the Great Smoky Mountains National Park, check out *Strangers in High Places, the Story of the Great Smoky Mountains*, by Michael Frome (University of Tennessee Press), *Historic Buildings of the Smokies*, by Ed Trout (Great Smoky Mountains Natural History Association), and *At Home in the Smokies* (U.S. Department of the Interior).

TOP SECRET

When making a stop at the Oconaluftee Park Service Visitor Center, don't miss the chance to walk down a short path from the center to the Mountain Farm Museum, a living history exhibit. Featured are a replica of an early southern Appalachian farm, free-roaming barnyard animals, and, from May through October, park personnel dressed in period costumes and performing typical farm chores of long ago. Admission is free.

Highways and Byways

10

Situated at the mouth of what became the Great Smoky Mountains National Park, Gatlinburg, Tennessee started out as a sleepy mountain retreat for the rich. As the park became more popular and tourist dollars flooded in, the town lost most of its tony feel and slowly succumbed to attractions like the Ripley's Believe It or Not Museum and the tramway to Ober Gatlinburg, an amusement park of sorts in the summer and a ski resort of sorts in the winter. The main parkway through town is segmented by ten stoplights. During the height of the vacation season, the traffic is stop and go à la *American Graffiti.* Of the 33,600 people in town on a typical summer day, 30,000 are tourists. Do you think those 3,600 or so year-round residents are going to spend all their time sitting in traffic?

The first secret route is the back way to get to Gatlinburg from I-40 in the north. Find your way onto U.S. Highway 411, the Dolly Parton Parkway, just east of the intersection of Chapman Highway (U.S. Highway 411/441) and Tennessee Highway 66 in Sevierville. Look for Pittman Center Road (Tennessee Highway 416) and head south. Keep going straight, even when the signs say that 416 turns to the left, and continue onto what has now become Birds Creek Road. (Sound confusing? We don't want to make it *too* easy.) Continue straight as the road becomes Buckhorn Road and ends at U.S. Highway 321. Take a right toward the west and follow U.S. Highway 321 into downtown Gatlinburg. Presto, you've now missed miles of traffic tie-ups along the main highway through Sevierville and Pigeon Forge.

Once you're in Gatlinburg, you have two options for getting around faster. On the east side, which is where the above route dumps you, you can pretty much avoid the main drag by turning from 321 onto Baskins Creek Bypass, then to Cherokee Orchard Road, and, finally, Airport Road. This takes you through lightly traveled parts of town and is a much quicker way to get to spots like the Roaring Fork Motor Nature Trail (Secret 26). A better-known alternative, but still less traveled than the main street on the other side of town, is River Road, which loops around from just after traffic light number 2 to U.S. Highway 441, heading toward the park's Sugarlands Visitor Center.

Finally, if you're coming through Pigeon Forge to the national park, you might want to skip Gatlinburg altogether. Just before you hit town on U.S. Highway 441, take the Gatlinburg Bypass. The road winds up through the mountains and deposits you outside town near the Sugarlands Visitor Center. Even if you want to see Gatlinburg, it's a good idea to take the bypass and sneak into town from the south side against all the heavy traffic that backs up coming from the north.

Secret Information

Secrets along the way: Arrowcraft Shop (Secret 54), Great Smoky Arts and Crafts Community (Secret 90), the Greenbrier Restaurant (Secret 77), Hippensteal's Mountain View Inn (Secret 3), House of Douglas Bakery (Secret 13), Roaring Fork Motor Nature Trail (Secret 26), the Soda Fountain (Secret 36).

TOP SECRET

If you're staying in a chalet or condo on Ski Mountain above Gatlinburg or are heading to Ober Gatlinburg, you can save time by taking the Gatlinburg Bypass rather than fighting your way through town. Just turn off at the exit to Campbell Lead Road and consult a map that shows the maze of winding roads on the mountaintop.

Locator Maps

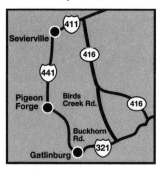

(Greater Gatlinburg Area)

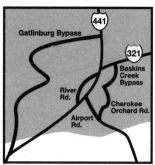

Blue Ridge Outing Company

Paddling the Tuckasegee

11

Bob Mattingly, owner of Blue Ridge Outing Company, built a family business by catering to families. In fact, no other outfitter in the Smokies will take kids as young as four for a rafting ride. "Nine out of ten people coming through that door are here to white-water raft with their kids," he observes. No, Mattingly isn't crazy. He just runs his operation on the Tuckasegee (the Cherokee word for "slow-moving turtle") River. The river runs mild instead of wild, and the little ones can enjoy white water without the wipeouts. All that said, we like to be that tenth person through the door who goes on an even more appealing family adventure by *canoeing* down the mild Tuckasegee.

Mattingly recently launched the first mild-water canoeing and kayaking operation on the North Carolina side of the Smokies. The six-and-a-half-mile paddling route parallels U.S. Highway 441/74, and it takes you past farms and campgrounds and over enough little ripples and rocks to make the ride interesting but harmless. Although Blue Ridge Outing offers guide-assisted canoe trips, nature and river ecology trips, and storyteller canoe trips, there is a lot to be said for going solo with your kids or friends. Say nothing or everything as you drift under blue skies gazing up at a red-tailed hawk soaring overhead. Sing to the beaver, otter, and occasional cow (hey, they get hot, too) soaking in the river. Finally, go at your own pace.

A Tennessee Valley Authority dam is situated several miles up the Tuckasegee. When the turbines at the dam are running, the water flows faster and higher downstream. When the turbines are off, however, the water level can get pretty low, especially during dry spells. So before making a canoe or kayak reservation, ask Blue Ridge Outing about the water level. Although a low water level can be slower and easier to maneuver through, too low a level means you'll be toting that canoe over the rocks in spots.

Most folks visit Blue Ridge during the summer, but fall is the time to canoe or kayak, Mattingly says. Not only do you stay warmer and drier in a canoe or kayak than on a raft, but the staff will have time to offer more special programs like storytelling trips. There's no better way to see the fall colors than floating down the tree-lined Tuckasegee in the middle of the mountains on a crisp, clear autumn day. Break out the flannel shirts and make a reservation early.

Secret Information

Location: Off U.S. Highway 441/74, halfway between Cherokee and Dillsboro, North Carolina.
Address: 7397 U.S. Highway 74 West, Whittier, North Carolina 28789.
Phone: (800) 572-3510 or (704) 586-3510.
Prices: Canoe and kayaks $10 for kids, $20 for adults.
Details: Blue Ridge Outing offers canoe and kayak instruction, but if you or your kids have been through a course at scout camp then you'll be fine. Everyone is outfitted with life jackets, and the equipment is all new. Pack a lunch in a backpack and bring along some drinks in a cooler, then along the way pick out a cove or patch of grass where you can stop and picnic.

TOP SECRET

Ask the folks at Blue Ridge Outing Company about scheduling a tour of the Second Chance Wildlife Rehabilitation Center in Whittier after your canoe trip. Blue Ridge staff member Russ Smith, an environmental specialist who runs the nature and ecology canoe trips, has volunteered several hours to the center, which helps care for injured and sick wild animals. The cost is $2.50 for adults and $1 for kids, and all fees go to help the animals at Second Chance.

A Dam Good Time

12

If you liked summer camp, you'll love Fontana Village in North Carolina. It's a place for families to stay and play in a setting that harks back to a simpler, slower-paced time.

There's a Mayberry spirit alive at Fontana, whether it's parents gathering on the softball field for a Saturday night, adults-only game or the kids who didn't know each other the day before racing around the grounds together like best buds. There are horseshoes and horseback riding, shuffleboard and swimming, miniature golf and tennis, basketball and bike rentals, archery and badminton, Ping-Pong and trout fishing—all either free or for a reasonable fee. There are escorted hikes, organized crafts classes, thirty miles of mountain bike trails, a swimming center with water slide, and an indoor pool, fitness facility, and arcade.

Over at Fontana Village marina, a couple of miles down North Carolina Highway 28, you can rent fully equipped houseboats, wave runners, pontoon boats, deck boats, and ski boats. To satisfy the monster appetite all this activity is bound to bring on, there's an ice cream parlor and three restaurants. The Village Grill features short-order favorites; the Peppermill Buffet House offers breakfast, lunch, and dinner buffets; and the Peppercorn Grill and Rib House serves as the only dress-nice-and-get-served eatery on the property. There's also a small grocery store, laundromat, gift shop, and post office, all within strolling distance from any cottage.

It's nice to have all that in one place, because Fontana is in the middle of nowhere, between the Great Smoky Mountains National Park to the north and the equally untamed Joyce Kilmer National Forest to the south. The village was created just weeks after Pearl Harbor in 1941, when the government decided it needed a new hydroelectric dam to power the nation's war effort. Almost overnight six thousand workers flooded into the area. Cottages were built to house the workmen and their families—along with a hospital, school, churches, and recreation facilities. When World War II ended, the men and their families left, but Fontana Village remained, and in the fifties it emerged as a vacation destination.

Accommodations are a tad spartan but comfortable. Some cottages look like they haven't worn well over the years, so be sure of what you're getting when you make reservations. The top-of-the-line Azalea models—three bedrooms and two baths, or two bedrooms and two baths—not only have new furnishings and appliances, but most have a fireplace and Jacuzzi bath (important if you plan to do any mountain bike riding). If you're looking for a simple, comfortable option without cooking facilities, then consider a room at the inn.

Secret Information

Location: Off North Carolina Highway 28, near the southwestern border of the Great Smoky Mountains National Park.

Address: P.O. Box 68, Highway 28, Fontana Dam, North Carolina 28733.

Phone: (800) 849-2258 or (704) 498-2211.

Rates: $59 to $189 for cottages; $49 to $149 for rooms at the inn; $20 per night for hookups with water and electricity, or $8 a night for tent camping at the campground.

Season: Cottages and hotel open year-round; campground open April 1 to November 1.

Credit cards: American Express, MasterCard, Visa.

TOP SECRET

Depending on your point of view, Fontana Dam, just east of Fontana Village, is a monument to man's ability to tame nature or a giant eyesore amid miles of unspoiled beauty. Either way, it's an impressive sight. Stop by the visitor center to learn how an army of workers rerouted a river to build it, then take a stroll atop the structure and fight vertigo as you look down hundreds of feet to the powerhouse below. By the way, the Appalachian Trail passes over the top of the structure.

A Taste of Britain

13

The House of Douglas Bakery is housed in a nondescript, easy-to-miss cinderblock and wood building in the Great Smoky Arts and Crafts Community (Secret 90) outside Gatlinburg, Tennessee. The interior is, to put it plainly, plain: three small two-person tables, shelves with a rather limited collection of cooking accessories and other knickknacks, and a glass display case where you give your order and pay. But then you notice the smell—freshly baked breads, authentic shortbread, and a variety of meat pies. Immediately, you forgive the rather modest atmosphere and start to crave what's certainly the best and, as far as we know, the only place to sample authentic Scottish food anywhere in the Smokies.

"We bake everything from scratch," says David Waddell, who owns the bakery with his wife, Linda. "People tell us that they come here because they miss the taste of freshly prepared 'real' foods."

David is from Scotland and spent fifteen years as a bush pilot in Kenya. He found his way to San Diego in the eighties, and he met and married Linda, an American of Irish descent, there. Her favorite spot in Southern California was Dudley's Bakery, and she dreamed of starting a similar business. David had always baked growing up, and the couple eventually moved to Oklahoma to open an Italian restaurant, where they started making struan bread. Customers bought more bread than spaghetti, so they decided to ditch the pasta and concentrate on baking.

They started baking goods to sell at the many gatherings for Scottish Highland Games and Celtic festivals around the country (caber tossing anyone?). They moved to Gatlinburg for its central location and relatively easy driving to states such as Texas, Florida, Michigan, New York, Virginia, and Indiana, where they sell food at festivals.

The Waddells opened the bakery to supplement their games'

income and serve whatever tourists happen to stop by. Drop in for an informal lunch and you can choose from a selection of delicious flaky pastry meat pies, chicken pot pies, sausage rolls, steak and vegetable pies, and steak and mushroom pies that conjure up images of a Glasgow pub. Most of the fare is Scottish, but they also occasionally prepare German and Swedish dishes. Be sure to take home a loaf of mission wheat bread or raisin bread as well as a slab or two of our favorite House of Douglas treat, wonderfully sweet shortbread. They also sell cinnamon pecan coffee cakes, scones, and fabulous cookies. Ask for free samples.

If you're in Gatlinburg in May, make time to attend the local Highland Games held at Mills Park. There are sheep dog demonstrations, battle ax-throwing, Highland wrestling, and haggis hurling. (If you don't know what haggis is, don't ask.) Look for David and Linda's red trailer, poke your head in, and say hello.

Secret Information

Location: On the Great Smoky Arts and Crafts Community loop, east of downtown Gatlinburg.

Address: 517 Glades Road, Gatlinburg, Tennessee 37738.

Phone: (423) 430-7568.

Hours: 8:00 P.M. to 5:00 P.M., Monday through Saturday (may vary based on how much business they get).

Prices: Breads $3 to $4 a loaf; pastries $1 to $1.50; meat pies $3.95.

Credit cards: None.

TOP SECRET

The House of Douglas Bakery is one of only a handful of places in the whole world that make struan bread—a mixture of wheat, corn, oats, brown rice, and bran, moistened with buttermilk and sweetened with brown sugar and honey. Scots traditionally made it out of whatever grains they had harvested for the feast of Saint Michael the Archangel. Delicious struan bread is on sale at the House of Douglas for $3 a loaf.

 **Secrets of Dollywood**

Good Golly Miss Dolly

14

With over two million guests in 1996, Dollywood was the second-most-visited attraction in Tennessee, behind only the Great Smoky Mountains National Park, so it can't exactly be called a secret. Here, however, is some inside information that might help you get more out of your visit to Dolly Parton's 118-acre theme park.

• The park, in Pigeon Forge, is filled with reminders of Dolly's past. Aunt Granny's Restaurant is named for the nickname given Dolly by her nieces and nephews. Apple Jack's Restaurant and Old Flames Candle Shop honor a pair of Dolly's hit records ("Apple Jack" and "Old Flames Can't Hold a Candle to You"). Pine's Theater is named for the Pines Theater in Sevierville, Tennessee, which was the site of Dolly's first public performance in the midfifties. Critter Creek Toy Factory recalls one of Dolly's grandpa's expressions: He called all the animals she played with as a child "critters." Red's Diner is named after the place where Dolly had her first hamburger, Red's in Sevierville. Uncle Bill's Guitar Shop is named for Dolly's uncle Bill Owens, who was her first manager and cowrote many of her songs. For a personal encounter with Dolly's past, visit awhile with Della Hurst, who makes lye soap in Craftsman's Valley. She was the first person to ever diaper the infant Dolly more than fifty years ago. Della can tell stories about the days before her now-famous friend had big, uh, hair.

• For special treats, check out the Dollywood Grist Mill, which is the only functioning hand-built gristmill constructed in Tennessee in the twentieth century. Fresh corn and wheat are ground daily, and the flour, meal, and baked goods are sold on-site. Or stop at the Hickory House for Dollywood's "special" barbecue. *Amusement Business* magazine cited it as the best pork barbecue served at any theme park in the nation. For fancier fare head to the Backstage Restaurant,

Fans flock to Dolly Parton's Tennessee Mountain Home, at Dollywood.
(Dollywood photo)

voted by *Southern Living* magazine as one of the top three eating establishments in the Smokies.

• To get the most for your money, buy a ticket to get into Dolly-wood after 3:00 P.M. and your next day's visit is free. In the summer, when the park stays open to 9:00 P.M., you can stay for six hours one day, then return the next day for the full twelve hours at no charge. This deal is good during the regular season, from April through the beginning of November. If you're spending a week or more in the area and plan to visit Dollywood a lot, then a season pass is a good investment: It costs less than two one-day tickets and it's also good for the Smoky Mountains Christmas celebration in November and December. Better yet, you don't have to decide whether to spring for the higher price until you've spent some time in the park. You can apply the price of your one-day ticket to the purchase of a season pass at the end of the day.

• To avoid most of the traffic pouring into Dollywood on a typical day during tourist season, take the back way to the parking lot (Secret 64). Another way to avoid the crowd is to head to Dollywood on a Thursday, which is typically its least busy day. Also, although the official opening time is 9:00 A.M., the gates really open at 8:30—take the hint, get there early, and beat the crowds.

Secret Information

Location:	Pigeon Forge, Tennessee.
Address:	1020 Dollywood Lane, Pigeon Forge, Tennessee 37863-4101.
Phone:	(423) 428-9400.
Prices (as of 1997):	$26.99 plus tax for a one-day adult ticket; $18.99 plus tax for a one-day child's ticket; $22.99 for a one-day senior ticket; kids, 3 and under, free; adult season passes $49.99; child's season pass $35.99.
Credit cards:	Discover, MasterCard.

TOP SECRET

Dollywood's craftsmen are genuine artisans, many of whom help preserve trades, like blacksmithing, that are part of our American heritage but no longer practiced much. From January to March, when the park is closed, many of the craftsmen hold workshops to give guests hands-on training in their respective trades. Master blacksmith Mike Rose, for example, conducts winter workshops to teach his craft and recently launched the first summer classes for both beginners and intermediates. The workshops are popular with locals and space is limited. For information, call Dollywood at (423) 428-9445.

15

Cultural Icons

Ken Blankenship, director of the Museum of the Cherokee Indian, is dismayed that the only examples of Native American culture seen by most tourists visiting Cherokee, North Carolina, are teepees and men in feathered headdresses from a John Wayne western. "The Cherokee people didn't live in teepees, but in cabins," he points out. "And they didn't wear those headdresses."

Bypass the bogus braves and check out the real story of the Cherokee at the museum. It's dedicated to telling the true story of the Qualla Boundary, the Cherokee reservation south of the Great Smoky Mountains National Park. The museum was recently renovated to give visitors a more interactive sense of the heritage of the tribe that once roamed 135,000 square miles from West Virginia to Alabama.

In the early 1800s the Cherokee ancestral homelands included the Smokies. When Europeans began establishing themselves there, one faction of the local tribe—led by legendary Chief Sequoyah—learned English and farming in an attempt to assimilate into white society. Some even owned slaves. Another group—the Oconoluftee—were appalled by their tribesmen's eagerness to ditch their native ways and seceded from the Cherokee nation. Then in 1838 the federal government signed a treaty that called for the Cherokee to leave their land and march twelve hundred miles along what became known as the Trail of Tears to Oklahoma. (One in four marchers died along the way.) But the dissident Oconoluftees' land was not considered part of the deal and they were allowed to stay put. They were joined by approximately a thousand Cherokee, who had hidden with their leader, Tsali, in the mountains during the relocation. Tsali traded his life (he was executed for killing a federal soldier shortly after his surrender) in exchange for a promise from the government that his people could remain on Cherokee soil. Tsali's followers and the Oconoluftee banded together

A statue of Chief Sequoyah greets visitors at the entrance to the Museum of the Cherokee Indian. (Photo courtesy of Museum of the Cherokee Indian)

to create the Eastern Band of the Cherokee Nation and run the reservation on which the tourist town of Cherokee now sits.

Despite its commercial surroundings, the museum does a wonderful job of educating visitors about the real history of the Cherokee. Of the recent renovation Blankenship says, "You will feel like you are there. It won't just be cases that you look in. You will be inside history." Displays cover ten thousand years of the past, including profiles of the twelve principal chiefs from the 1800s to the present. Current chief Joyce Elaine Conseen is the first woman to hold the position. Audio and visual presentations tell Cherokee legends about the creation of fire, the mountains, the earth, and the Milky Way. Other exhibits focus on a 250-year-old canoe, war masks, baskets, pottery, and tools. Visitors can also walk through outdoor replicas of two fifteenth-century Native American dwellings. The whole thing is an eye-opening experience and worth wading through parts of Cherokee to see.

Secret Information

Location: U.S. Highway 441, at Drama Road in downtown Cherokee.

Address: P.O. Box 1599, Cherokee, North Carolina 28719.

Phone: (704) 497-3481.

Hours: 9:00 A.M. to 8:00 P.M., Monday through Saturday; 9:00 A.M. to 5:00 P.M., Sunday, mid-June through August; 9:00 A.M. to 5:00 P.M., Sunday and Monday the rest of the year.

Prices: $4 for adults; $2 for children.

Credit cards: American Express, Discover, MasterCard, Visa.

TOP SECRET

For another entertaining taste of true Native American tradition besides the Museum of the Cherokee Indian, head for *Unto These Hills.* The acclaimed outdoor drama tells the story of the Cherokee from the time of the Spanish explorer Hernando de Soto in 1540 to the tribe's 1838 forced migration along the Trail of Tears. First presented in 1950, the production is staged nightly, except Sunday, from June through late August at the Mountainside Theater on Drama Road in Cherokee. Admission is $5 to $12.

Christy

Hollywood in the Smokies

16

The North Carolina side of the Smokies has been the location for Hollywood productions like *The Fugitive*. Likewise, the Tennessee side has had a starring role on-screen in the television show *Christy*. Shot in and around Townsend, the program, which aired on CBS during 1992–93, is based on Catherine Marshall's classic tale of a young, turn-of-the-century woman who came to Appalachia to teach in a one-room schoolhouse. While fictional, the book is based on the real-life experience of Marshall's mother. It describes the dramatic story of Christy Huddleston's attempts to educate children who came to school—*when* they came to school—shoeless and with empty stomachs.

The book is actually set in Del Rio, Tennessee, but the producers found that area too remote for equipment and trucks. Instead, they chose to shoot in the shadow of the Smokies. The series took the premise of the book and gave it a bit of a soap opera feel by focusing not only on the trials of teaching poverty-stricken kids but on the love triangle between Kellie Martin (who got her big break in the series *Life Goes On*), the Bible-thumping young preacher, and the atheist local doctor. Other key characters were played by Tyne Daly (*Cagney and Lacy*), Tess Harper (*Tender Mercies*), and LeVar Burton (*Star Trek: The Next Generation*). For a while, eating at local spots like Chef Jock's Tastebuds Cafe (Secret 92) was like dining with the stars at Spago. Sadly, however, the series never drew the high ratings network execs pine for, and it was canceled after twenty or so episodes.

Christy lives on in the Smokies, though. As a souvenir of your vacation, you can take home videos of several episodes and relive the splendid scenery of the mountains while sampling some well-acted melodrama. Also (we shouldn't tell you this, so keep it to yourself), you can get a firsthand look at some of the locations at

Christy *series star Kellie Martin poses with an extra, obviously an admirer, on the set of the show.*

which the series was filmed—but only from a distance. The main set with the little wooden church/one-room schoolhouse still stands down an unassuming backroad just a long spit into Wears Valley. From Townsend, head northeast on U.S. Highway 321 (Secret 55) toward Pigeon Forge. Cross over the little bridge and keep your eyes peeled on the left for Rudd Hollow Road. Turn left and stay to the right when Rudd Hollow splits. You're now on Lizzie Lane. Veer right when the road splits again and look to your left for a clearing in which the wooden church/schoolroom featured in the series is visible atop a gentle slope.

The main set for the program sits on property owned by the Abbott family, who leased roughly eighteen acres of their family homestead to *Christy*'s producers. The children's swing also still stands in the field where many scenes were filmed, including the shot during the opening credits of Kellie Martin doing cartwheels. Also on the land, but not visible from the road, are the mission house and the doctor's cabin. The view from the road is about as close as you can get to the set, however; it's on private property and no trespassing is allowed.

Continue on and follow Dunn Hollow Road (a public school bus route that ends back on U.S. Highway 321) right past a barn that was painted to look like the fictional Del Rio post office and the house that was used as the Spencer cabin, home to Tess Harper's character in the series. Across the road is the Abbotts' house, so don't go snooping around on their property.

Secret Information

Christy videos are available at the Townsend Visitors Center for $20 each or three for $50 and six for $100. To order the complete *Christy* series on video, call Time-Life Video at (800) 245-8181. The first installment is $4.99; additional episodes, which are mailed monthly, are $19.95 plus $3.49 shipping and handling. There's also a *Christy* fan club web site at www.alt.tv.christy.

TOP SECRET

For serious fans who want to take home some *Christy* collectibles (sorry, there are no *Christy* lunch boxes or action figures that we know of), head to the Museum of Appalachia in Norris (Secret 47). John Rice Irwin, the museum's creator, bought several items from Ken Wales, the program's executive producer, that were used as props in the show. The *Christy* collection is for sale upstairs in the museum gift shop. Other items are scattered around the first floor. Prices range from a few bucks for a children's book to a few hundred for antique furnishings. Call the museum at (423) 494-7680.

Drug Story

Turning onto Gay Street in the heart of Dandridge, founded in 1783 and the second-oldest town in Tennessee, is like returning to small-town America of the thirties. Protected by the "million dollar dike" (the sodded earth and rock dike President Franklin D. Roosevelt ordered built in 1942 to save Dandridge from being annihilated when Douglas Dam was built), the town square is dotted with brick buildings that retain their turn-of-the-century facades. There's a hardware store, used-appliance store, jeweler, florist, attorney's office, and the Tinsley-Bible Drug Company, a classic drugstore straight out of a Frank Capra film.

The store, named after two of its previous owners—Dr. P. A. Tinsley and Lloyd "Doc" Bible—opened in 1911. Not much about the feel of it has changed since then. Sure, it now sells the same toothpastes and shampoos as your local Wal-Mart, and the pharmacy is computerized; but the atmosphere is strictly retro. There are old-style, floor-to-ceiling wood shelving and display cases, and the decor is littered with old jars and bottles, farm implements such as a hand scythe, a ceramic bedpan, and a hand meat grinder. These touches aren't calculated country chic; rather, they seem a natural part of the place. A display case in back is stuffed with a fascinating collection of old medicines and other products that the current owner salvaged when he took over—Deluxe Bay Rum (57 percent alcohol, for external use only), bed-bug liquid (kills bed bugs and roaches), beef iron and wine, Oriole brand North Carolina pine tar, wormwood oil, and Lee's Save the Baby Cough Suppressant.

Tinsley-Bible is one of the last places we know where you can sit down at an old-fashioned drugstore lunch counter and get a hamburger for $1.29. Also available are chicken and dumplings for $1.45 and a milk shake for $1.17. The eating area is tiny, with six stools and seven small booths. The walls behind the counter are covered with family photos, diplomas, and cornpone sentiments like "It's better to keep your mouth shut and appear stupid than to open it and remove all doubt."

The food is basic—beans and corn bread, hot dogs with chili and slaw, turkey sandwiches—and it's served on wax paper or in plain ceramic bowls. But getting a bite at Tinsley-Bible isn't about eating; it's about spending a few minutes eavesdropping on conversations, soaking up the atmosphere, and imagining that you are back in a simpler time and place.

Secret Information

Location: Downtown Dandridge, Tennessee.
Address: 1224 Gay Street, Dandridge, Tennessee 37725.
Phone: (423) 397-3444.
Hours: 8:00 A.M. to 6:00 P.M., Monday through Friday; 8:00 A.M. to 3:00 P.M., Saturday.
Credit cards: Discover, MasterCard, Visa.

TOP SECRET

Across the street from the Tinsley-Bible Drug Company is the Jefferson County Courthouse, built in 1845 and listed on the National Register of Historic Places. Inside is a folksy little community museum opened to the public in 1958. The dozen or so display cases contain an eclectic collection of Confederate, Native American, and Appalachian artifacts donated by locals. Items include the marriage license of Davy Crockett and Polly Finley, a circa-1930 copy of the *Great Smoky Mountains National Park Guide*, a moonshine still, and a mound of Confederate bills. Admission is free and the museum is open when the courthouse is—Monday through Friday, 8:00 A.M. until 4:00 P.M.; and Saturday, 8:00–11:00 A.M.

18

A Vacation Wonderland

For decades the Wonderland Lodge was the only hotel inside the Great Smoky Mountains National Park. Situated in the Elkmont area on the Tennessee side of the park, it was built in 1912 to shelter loggers harvesting timber nearby. When the area became a part of the national park, the hotel became a favorite destination for tourists who wanted to stay in the wilderness without giving up all the comforts of home. The lodge's lease ran out in 1992 and it closed. Today, the twenty-five-room structure is slowly crumbling, caught between those who want to tear it down and those who want to preserve it as a historic building.

The last general manager of the Wonderland, however, wanted to keep the hotel alive. Daryl Husky scoured the area for another site on which to re-create the ambiance of an old-time mountain lodge. He finally found it in Wears Valley, just a stone's throw from the border of the Great Smoky Mountains National Park. There he built a close reproduction of the old Wonderland.

The hotel is short on frills and long on peace, quiet, and hospitality. Its twenty-nine rooms are furnished with just the basics: beds, a dresser, and a night table. Each room has a small bath, which is an improvement on the old hotel, which required some guests to share a bathroom down the hall. There are no telephones and no televisions.

The hotel doesn't advertise because about 90 percent of its guests are repeat customers. They come back to sit in the rocking chairs or swings on the football-field-long wooden front porch, where they can enjoy the view of Cove Mountain. There's a horseshoe pit on the front lawn and a small game room with a pool table in back of the lobby, but few other diversions (kids might get bored).

As accommodations in the Smokies go, the Wonderland is relatively affordable and in a prime location. It's only nine miles from Pigeon Forge, five miles from Townsend, and two miles to the back entrance of the national park (Secret 55). As Roy, the desk clerk who

The Wonderland Hotel offers a wonderful front-porch setting for relaxation.

has greeted guests for years, says, "It's away from everything, but it's easy to get to any place you want."

Secret Information

Location: Off Lines Spring Road, south of U.S. Highway 321 in Wears Valley.
Address: 3889 Wonderland Way, Sevierville, Tennessee 37862.
Phone: (423) 428-0779.
Rates: $41 to $71 per room; $105 to $115 per cabin.
Season: Mid-March through November and during the week after Christmas. Reservations are accepted starting October 15 for the following season.
Credit cards: American Express, Discover, MasterCard, Visa.

TOP SECRET

You don't have to stay overnight to enjoy the Wonderland Hotel. The restaurant behind swinging screen doors off the lobby serves such true-blue southern breakfasts, lunches, and dinners as gravy and biscuits, pinto beans and corn bread, and mountain trout. Stop by for a filling meal, grab a Mason jar of iced tea, and feel free to sit a spell on the hotel's huge front porch.

Mild Kingdom

Since opening Smoky Mountain Deer Farm and Exotic Petting Zoo with little more than a dream and a small herd of deer, Greg and Lynn Hoisington have continually expanded their farm. It now includes more than one hundred Mediterranean and Japanese deer plus a wide array of exotic animals ranging from pure white New Zealand wallabies to the mop-topped, copper-colored Scottish Highland cattle, and from miniature horses to proud peacocks that strut freely around the barnyard road.

Unlike most other petting zoos, which cram several goats, a couple deer, and maybe a llama in a gated pen, the farm, near Sevierville, Tennessee, features individual enclosures that closely resemble each animal's natural habitat. Clark the llama (who, incidentally, spits when petted) resides in a shaded hillside setting that offers plenty of leafy vegetation and ample opportunity for climbing. The ferret family, which can be observed but not touched because of their sharp teeth, also has an imaginative living area consisting of multilevel pens and tunnels made from white PVC tubing.

The big attraction for small fries, of course, is being able to pet and feed animals they might have only seen in videos or through the Plexiglas at a zoo. The Hoisingtons' animals are clean, well cared for, and tame. Not only has the farm been inspected and approved each year by the USDA and the AAA Travel Club, but the Sevier County Humane Department officials and local veterinarians work in partnership with the Hoisingtons to help ensure that all of the animals remain healthy. Rules and information are posted on each animal enclosure telling what and how to feed, whether to pet or not, and a brief background on the breed.

Animal feed is extra and is best purchased for $3.50 in a huge plastic souvenir cup at the gift shop. The thirty-two-ounce mixture of corn and chow will feed most of the animals in the park and can easily last your whole visit. Sliced apples for the reindeer and horses are

This potbelly would appreciate a twenty-five-cent investment in the feed machine on the right.

available at the central refill station for fifty cents. Potbellies and camels eat chow that's stored in gumball-type machines and costs a quarter a handful. You could simply see the animals and mingle with the gentle fallow deer and the miniature pygmy goats (the two enclosures that visitors are allowed to enter). On the other hand, there's nothing quite like having a massive Scottish Highland bull with longhorns gently nuzzle your palm, the hoofed highlight of any trek to the deer farm.

Secret Information

Location: On U.S. Highway 411, east of downtown Sevierville.

Address: 478 Happy Hollow Lane, Sevierville, Tennessee 37876.

Phone: (423) 428-DEER (3337).

Hours: 10:00 A.M. until 7:00 P.M. (5:00 P.M., November through April).

Season: Year-round except Thanksgiving, Christmas, and the first week of January.

Prices: Adults $5; seniors $4.50; children, 3–12, $3, and 2 and under, free. Animal feed is extra and ranges from 25¢ for a handful of chow to $3.50 for a refillable (for $1.50) 32-ounce souvenir cup.

Credit cards: Discover, MasterCard, Visa.

TOP SECRET

On a hilltop overlooking the Smoky Mountain Deer Farm and Exotic Petting Zoo is the Deer Farm Riding Stables, also owned and operated by the Hoisingtons. The half-hour ($10) and hour ($15) rides over gentle, ten-foot-wide trails are ideal for novice riders and offer unobstructed views of the Smokies and the surrounding valley. All trips are led by a guide, and several treks are escorted by the area's only riding trail guide pig: Snortin' Norton knows all the trails plus the all-important shortcuts, which can really save a portly little pig on a winding four-mile, hour-long trip.

The Ol' Swimmin' Hole

20

Water is the lifeblood of the Smokies. Starting at the top of the peaks that form the ridge of the Appalachians, an average of eighty inches of rain a year floods, flows, rushes, rambles, rolls, crashes, cascades, streams, sluices, surges, pours, drifts, trickles, and gushes down the mountainsides. The H_2O nourishes a greater diversity of flora and fauna (Secrets 30 and 71) than can be found almost anywhere else in the United States and shapes some of the most beautiful sites in the area: towering waterfalls, boulder-strewn streams, and crystal-clear pools.

Traveling alongside one of the Great Smoky Mountains National Park's countless streams on a hot, humid summer day, you're likely to get an uncontrollable urge to stop and plunge in—with or without a bathing suit. Go ahead. Swimming is permitted anywhere in the park (but please don't skinny-dip). There are turnoffs all over the place where you can pull over the car, scramble down the creek bank, and cool off in a secluded swimming hole.

Our favorite out-of-the-way spot to take the family for a summer swim is Big Creek, which is situated smack-dab on the Tennessee–North Carolina border at the northeast corner of the national park. Just below a small metal bridge spanning the stream at the parking and picnic area is a great place to splash and slosh around in relatively shallow water—there's only one small spot where it gets too deep for adults to stand in. A small ledge offers a nice place to sit in the sun, and smaller kids like to slide into the pool from it. Up the bank are plenty of picnic tables, each next to a grill, where you can break out the burgers, hot dogs, potato salad, and watermelon. One of the streamside sites is even wheelchair accessible.

A couple of warnings about taking a dip at Big Creek or anywhere else in the park. First, even on the hottest days the water is going to be a bit brisk. The shade from towering trees and the swiftly moving water, even in spots that look calm, keep average water temperatures chilly. Second, swimming in the Smokies isn't like taking a dip in the motel pool. This is the wilderness (that's the whole point of a national park), and swimming can be dangerous: The current can get powerful; rocks are slippery; and certain spots might be deceivingly deep. There are no lifeguards on duty, and medical help might be miles away. Be careful and use common sense. Some daredevils, for example, like to climb up onto rock outcroppings and jump twenty or thirty feet into the water; they're just asking to star on *Rescue 911*. Swim smart. Swim safe. Come on in, the water's fine.

Secret Information

Location: Off I-40 (exit 451), about two miles past the Carolina Power and Light Company plant on the Big Pigeon River.

For more information about Big Creek or swimming in the Smokies, contact the Great Smoky Mountains National Park at (423) 436-1200.

TOP SECRET

If Big Creek is too crowded or too tame a swimming hole for your tastes, head up the Big Creek Trail for a mile-and-a-half hike to Midnight Hole. The fifty-foot-wide pool sits at the base of a small waterfall and ranges in depth from one to twelve feet. Fewer people find their way there than to the area near the Big Creek Campground. The water is deeper, and it's also a bit more hazardous, so be careful.

A River Runs Through It

21

Mark Twain complained that "golf is a good walk spoiled." Maybe the former riverboat pilot would have better appreciated the grand old game if the courses he played had a river like something out of a Twain tale running right through them. River Islands stretches over 220 acres and across three islands in the French Broad River near Kodak, Tennessee. It offers something for everyone, from scratch golfers to scenery watchers, by being one of the most challenging and beautiful courses in the state.

Golf Digest gave River Islands a four-star "worth planning your vacation around" rating, the highest of any public course in East Tennessee. Overall, the magazine ranks it ninth among all links in the state and second among public courses. Designed by the fabled Arthur Hills, who also created the Palmetto Dunes course on Hilton Head Island, it is a European-style "links" course (nine holes out and nine holes back, rather than the American practice of weaving the front and back nine holes to and from the clubhouse). Its varying terrain and natural hazards (five of the course's holes span the three islands in the river) challenge every aspect of even an experienced golfer's game. Everyone, including the heartiest hackers, should plan to rent a cart rather than carry or wheel their bags. Fortunately, the combined greens and cart fee are extremely affordable when compared to other top-notch golf courses.

Even if you have never broken 100 (shots, that is, not clubs), you can have a great time driving, pitching, and putting your way around River Islands. The scenery is spectacular, although you shouldn't expect to see the manicured grounds of Augusta National. Here, wildlife is everywhere. You're more likely to have your swing thrown off by the honk of a Canada goose than a Chrysler, or to slice a bad shot toward a grazing cow than a million-dollar house with a fairway view. The links are lined with black-eyed Susans, azaleas, oaks, and other greenery. October, when golfers risk being distracted by the blazing color of the turning trees, and May, when the wildflowers are blooming, are the busiest times on the course, a favorite of repeat visitors from Ohio and Michigan. Some people, in fact, come to River Islands not to play but to hitch rides with players and just tour the course in golf carts.

Secret Information

Location: Off I-40 (exit 402), in Kodak, Tennessee.
Address: 9610 Kodak Road, Kodak, Tennessee 37764.
Phone: (800) 34RIVER or (423) 933-0100.
Prices: $36 to $48 (includes cart and tax).
Credit cards: American Express, MasterCard, Visa.

TOP SECRET

If you're going to play River Islands Golf Club, bring along John Daly's swing and your Big Bertha driver when you hit hole number six. This baby was named the ninth-toughest hole in the region by *East Tennessee Golf News* because it offers the dual hazard of overwhelming length—639 yards from the back tee—and water all along the left side. No other hole on the eighteen-toughest list came close to River Islands' number six in terms of distance. The trick, of course, is to drive long without hooking it into the water. Easier said than done.

Express Lanes

22

We're not sure why most people coming east from Nashville or west from Asheville to the Tennessee side of the Smokies on Interstate 40 get off at exit 407, then head south on Tennessee Highway 66 through Sevierville toward the mountains. With its miles of billboards, tourist attractions, and bumper-to-bumper traffic, that route is certainly not the most scenic or most pleasant. It isn't even the fastest.

If you don't want to waste time and money from either direction, jump off I-40 well before exit 407 and take a less commercial drive to the Smokies. One option is U.S. Highway 321 (Secret 55). A more direct way from the interstate to the mountains, however, is the east-west route formed by Chapman Highway out of Knoxville on the west and Newport Highway out of Newport on the east.

Coming from the west, the route starts in downtown Knoxville. Take the exit for U.S. Highway 441 South, pass through the tunnel, and you'll drive right by the 1982 World's Fair symbol, the Sunsphere, which looks like a giant golf ball perched atop a tee. Continue south on Chapman Highway/U.S. Highway 441 across the river, noting that off to your right is the University of Tennessee's Neyland Stadium, home to the Tennessee Volunteers, which is almost always filled to capacity with 105,000 spectators on game day.

The road, named after Lonas B. Chapman, travels through South Knoxville, merging with U.S. Highway 411 just south of the small community of Seymour. Drive a few more miles and you'll hit the junction of Chapman Highway/U.S. Highway 441/411 and Tennessee Highway 66. Once there you'll be thrilled to see all the folks who took the I-40, exit 407, route backed up in traffic at the stoplight. You can now follow U.S. Highway 441 south through Sevierville. Or you can continue straight east on U.S. Highway 411 (the Dolly Parton Parkway) and in a few minutes take the back way to Gatlinburg (Secret 10) or Pigeon Forge (Secret 64).

Coming from the east, get off at exit 432 at Newport and follow

U.S. Highway 411 south, also known as Newport Highway. There aren't many attractions along the way, but that's precisely the point. Rather than get caught in Touristland, you'll get a chance to get a true taste of life in East Tennessee. The road rambles past modest homes, falling-down barns, charming churches, working farms, community stores, and even the huge factory where Bush Brothers packages its cans of beans. As you approach Sevierville, things get a bit more commercial but not overwhelming, and you can choose to take the shortcuts to Pigeon Forge and Gatlinburg mentioned above before hitting the jammed-up junction with Tennessee Highway 66.

Secret Information

Secrets along the way: The Laurel Theater (Secret 73), Smoky Mountain Deer Farm and Exotic Petting Zoo (Secret 19), and Ye Olde Steakhouse (Secret 98).

TOP SECRET

If traveling from Knoxville to the mountains on Chapman Highway, you can avoid all the traffic lights of Sevierville, Pigeon Forge, and Gatlinburg by turning right at White's School Road, which starts about nine miles south of the junction of U.S. Highway 411 and U.S. Highway 441 in Seymour. Follow White's School about a half mile to Goose Gap Road. Take a right and travel Goose Gap as it winds about five miles through the foothills to Walden's Creek Road. Go straight across Walden's Creek to Old Valley Road and follow it just under a mile as it veers left to become Russie Gap Road. The shortcut ends on U.S. Highway 321 in Wears Valley. Head left to Pigeon Forge or right to the Wears Valley entrance to the Great Smoky Mountains National Park or Townsend.

Locator Map

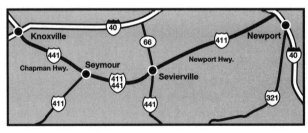

Mountain Memories

Barn Razing

23

Anyone who drives the country lanes surrounding the Great Smoky Mountains National Park will spot at least a dozen leaning, leaking, lonesome old barns. To some they're quaint. To others they're trash. But to an enterprising Maggie Valley, North Carolina, couple and their son, potential treasure is buried in the worn boards of those tired old buildings.

The Hornick family—Ray and Sam and their married son, Jason—tear down and haul off old barns, fence posts, and other bits of wood and barbed wire discarded by their neighbors. They get some weird looks from the locals (especially from the guys down at the sawmill)—that is, until the skeptics see the one-of-a-kind wooden souvenirs and distinctive mountain furniture the Hornicks create from the ruins. The family's recycled works of art are on display in their creekside studio, Mountain Memories. On most days Sam can be found there painting country scenes on old wood or antique saw blades, while Ray, a veteran general contractor from Florida, is in the back with his loyal companion, an Alaskan Malamute named Kesheika, lovingly handcrafting lamps, mantels, tables, and chairs.

"It's a real gamble when we tear down a barn," says Jason, who co-owns Mountain Memories with his mom and dad. "Sometimes we get wormy chestnut, hickory, or oak, and other times it's all junk and we can't use it. I spend most of the winter driving around looking for wood. Most people don't realize what they have and will let you have it for free if you haul it away. Other people think they have gold, when they probably have garbage."

Reclaiming old barns isn't as easy as stacking wood in the back of a pickup, however. "If a barn has fallen down, then the cows poop all over the wood," Sam says. "There was one time we had to load it on the truck and run it through the car wash to get the cow mess off."

Old barn wood can be nicely recycled in a number of ways, even for floral displays.

Even fairly clean wood has to be planed in the shop to see what lurks beneath the weathered exterior. The Hornicks concentrate their search on barns built in the thirties, when chestnut trees were plentiful in the area. According to Sam, a blight during the depression killed off the area's chestnuts, so the wood used to build the old barns is priceless. Barns built in the fifties are always a surprise, since farmers building barns used portable sawmills and cut down whatever was closest to the pasture. One board could be poplar, another oak, another pine, and still another hickory. It all depends on what trees were on hand at building time.

Whether the old wood turns out to be treasure or trash, none of it goes to waste at Mountain Memories. Wood that's not suitable for furniture is often turned into birdhouse-sized North Carolina tobacco barns, which have authentic tin roofs made from recycled cans donated by local restaurants.

"People come to the mountains and bring back a souvenir made in Taiwan or something made of oak that's churned out by the thousands at a factory," Sam adds, while holding one of the distinctive candleholders she made from a fence post Jason saved from a friend's woodpile. "We can't compete with the big companies, so we decided to do something unique. With our pieces, people can take home a souvenir that's not only from the mountains, it's of the mountains. We say, 'We recycle history into a mountain memory.' "

Secret Information

Location: On U.S. Highway 19, in Maggie Valley, North Carolina.

Address: 4956 Soco Road, Maggie Valley, North Carolina 28751.

Phone: (704) 926-5050.

Hours: 10:00 A.M. to 5:00 P.M., Friday through Sunday, and weekdays by appointment.

Prices: From $20 for a distinctive cutting board handmade from oak, walnut, and poplar to $1,000 or more for a harvest-type dining room table.

Credit cards: MasterCard, Visa.

TOP SECRET

Mountain Memories' owners, Ray and Sam Hornick, belong to the subculture of Maggie Valley, North Carolina, residents known as "halfbacks." That's the term locals have bestowed upon people who were raised in the northern tier of states, moved to Florida, and now have retired or, in the Hornicks' case, semiretired halfway back to the North in the Carolina mountains. Mountain Memories has a loyal halfback clientele, who call upon the collective creative genius of Ray and Sam to furnish and decorate their new mountainside retirement homes and vacation cabins in rustic style. "They're sick of the white and pastel Florida furniture. Besides, it would look pretty ugly in the log cabins," Sam says. Ray Hornick will custom-craft a piece for you, or you can purchase directly from the in-store display.

24

Proud to Be Americans

The patriotic heart of small-town America beats behind all the faux-alpine glitter and glow in Gatlinburg, Tennessee. Home folks and the tourists attracted to the mountain town are red, white, and blue to the core. On no other day is this more apparent, of course, than the Fourth of July, when Gatlinburg decorates every porch, post, and light pole in the colors of Old Glory.

Gatlinburg locals pack all the action they can muster into Independence Day. That's why they kick off their celebration at one minute past midnight with the nation's first, as in earliest, Fourth of July Parade. This annual extravaganza attracts an estimated one hundred thousand visitors each year. People pack the parkway two and three deep in spots to glimpse floats carrying performers from favorite local tourist attractions (like Elmwood Smooch's Hillbilly Hoedown and the Dixie Stampede), pint-sized versions of the helium character balloons hoisted in Macy's Thanksgiving Day Parade, and marching bands from local high schools.

Don't get the idea, however, that Gatlinburg's parade is on the scale of slicker nighttime productions such as Miami's King Orange or Disney World's electrical parades. Gatlinburg's unique Fourth of July Parade is pure Mayberry-after-midnight, complete with homemade floats hauled by pickups, fresh-faced church groups, and every local beauty pageant queen from miles around, each riding in brightly polished big American cars from the nearby Chevy and Ford dealerships.

The procession starts on the north end of the Gatlinburg Parkway (the end closest to Pigeon Forge) and breaks up about an hour later at the entrance to the Great Smoky Mountains National Park. Folks start lining up around 10:00 P.M. armed with lawn chairs, blankets, and coolers (nonalcoholic beverages only) to get a good spot and to "people watch." We enjoy watching the unofficial parade of vacationers of every size, shape, and hairdo almost as much as the main event itself.

Although Gatlinburg's version offers standard small-town America parade fare, the midnight starting time not only electrifies the floats and the crowd, everyone is nicely cooled by the mountain night air. Crowd favorites include the original Bat Boat and Bat Cycle on loan from Gatlinburg's Star Cars, authentic Tennessee Walking Horses, traditional Scottish bagpipers in their tartan kilts, and more than a dozen zipping and zooming Shriners in minirace cars and midget semitrucks. Most amazing of all, however, are the homegrown girl cloggers who somehow manage to hop and kick in moving flatbeds without hurtling painfully to the pavement. That's one you simply have to see for yourself.

Secret Information

Location: On the Gatlinburg Parkway through Gatlinburg, Tennessee.
Date: July 4.
Time: 12:01 A.M.
Phone: (800) 568-4748 or (423) 430-4148.

TOP SECRET

With an estimated one hundred thousand packing the parkway for the Gatlinburg Fourth of July Parade, it's smartest to sneak into town from the back side through the Great Smoky Mountains National Park. If you're coming from Sevierville, Pigeon Forge, or Townsend, take U.S. Highway 321 through Wears Valley and enter the park through the back entrance near Metcalf Bottoms Campground (Secret 55). Then hang a left and head toward Gatlinburg. Park as close to the park entrance as possible to expedite your exit at 1:00 A.M.

25

Hey, Dude

The Cherokee can say in one melodic word what it would take a complete English sentence to describe. One of the best examples of their linguistic prowess is the word *cataloochee*, which means "wave upon wave." If you drive all the way up Fie Top Road in Maggie Valley, North Carolina, you'll immediately understand just what that means. Where the road ends is where Cataloochee Ranch begins. From there all you can see for miles in every direction is wave upon wave of mist-covered mountains.

For easterners who have only dreamed of a western dude ranch vacation, Cataloochee Ranch is a more-than-palpable alternative to heading all the way out to Arizona or Colorado. It sits a mile high on one thousand acres of some of the area's most pristine pastureland and woodlands. The mountains beyond—none other than the Great Smoky Mountains National Park—can be reached by guests via three private entrances located on the ranch property. The undisturbed surroundings offer limitless possibilities for hiking, horseback riding, wildflower walking, bird watching, and, in the winter, downhill skiing at Cataloochee Ski Area (Secret 82), which is situated just one mile away.

The Alexander family, which has operated the place since Tom and "Miss Judy" Alexander opened the first Cataloochee dude ranch down in the valley in 1934 (it moved to its present location in 1938), specializes in the cowboy brand of pampering found only at the country's finest guest ranches. The modified American plan includes bountiful breakfasts and hearty family-style dinners that would satisfy the weariest wrangler. The ranch's vegetable gardens provide only the freshest ingredients for each meal, and "steak-outs" (outdoor barbecues) are held frequently on pleasant days. Dessert is topped with a double dose of spectacular natural majesty—burnt-orange sunsets followed by a midnight black sky dotted with a sea of stars.

With hayrides, campfires, galloping horses, and grazing cows,

The view from Cataloochee Ranch is the epitome of the mist-covered Smoky Mountains. (M. Nevros photo courtesy of Cataloochee Ranch)

Cataloochee sure looks like a working ranch—and the fresh-faced, cowboy-booted wranglers, servers, and housekeepers do bust their butts keeping everyone happy. But for the guests, Cataloochee Ranch is about as far removed from work as one can get. It's luxurious and laid back. There's a twenty-foot heated swim spa, and every room—whether in the main Ranch House, Silverbell Lodge, or in one of the cabins or suites—is decorated in an Eddie Bauer-esque, high-quality rustic style. The log beams are beaming. The quilts are handmade. The copper pots and ladles are polished, and the couches are made of perfectly worn leather. Stepping into the main Ranch House is like dying and going to *Bonanza* heaven.

Secret Information

Location: About three miles west of Maggie Valley, North Carolina.

Address: Route 1, Box 500, Maggie Valley, North Carolina 28751.

Phone: (800) 868-1401 or (704) 926-1401.

Fax: (704) 926-9249.

Rates: Lodging options range from rooms with full bath in the main Ranch House at $130 per night for two (including breakfast and dinner) to $355 per night for four in the Laurel Cabin, a two-story, remodeled original log cabin with a fireplace, kitchenette, a loft and main floor bedroom, and a footed tub under a skylight.

Details: Minimum stays are required at certain times of the year and one-night stays are discouraged.

Credit cards: American Express, MasterCard, Visa.

TOP SECRET

Even if you can't afford to stay overnight at Cataloochee Ranch, you can still share the dude ranch experience by joining a morning, afternoon, or all-day horseback ride there. Trails lead through fields of wildflowers and rhododendron tunnels, across lush forests and pastures, and along babbling streams. There are plenty of mountaintop vistas along the way, whether your ride traverses ranch property or meanders through the Great Smoky Mountains National Park. Half-day rides, which leave at 9:30 A.M. and 2:30 P.M. daily cost $35 for ranch guests and $40 for the public. Full-day rides, which are scheduled upon request and include lunch, cost $80 for guests and $85 for everyone else. One-hour horseback lessons are also available for $35. And the ranch offers periodic four- or six-day horse packing trips that are designed to allow riders to experience life as it was for settlers in the early days of the Cataloochee Valley.

Roaring Fork Motor Nature Trail

Car Trek

It's a shame that most people heading to the Great Smoky Mountains National Park through Gatlinburg, Tennessee, never bother to venture off the main drag. Turn onto Airport Road at stoplight number 8 and you're on your way to a drive that's a sampler of all the best the park has to offer. Better yet, it only takes a couple hours, and when you're done you end up back in town rather than somewhere out in the wild.

Touring the Roaring Fork Motor Nature Trail is like hiking in the comfort of your car. Nature is only a few feet away as you drive the paved one-lane road that climbs five miles up and down the mountains through chestnut oaks, white oaks, magnolias, maples, sweet birches, hemlocks, yellow poplars, and pines. Small bridges span rushing boulder-strewn creeks that carry water from Mount LeConte, the tallest peak in the park. Just off the road are the abandoned homesteads of people who first settled in the area 150 years ago and who traveled the same path on foot, horseback, or in wagons. Top speed is about fifteen miles an hour, although all the twists and turns keep the driver awake. It's a great drive on a hot day—the temperature drops about ten degrees or so from the bottom to the top of the route, thanks to the shade of the dense forest and change in elevation.

There are spots to stop and stretch your legs and explore the homesteads of early settlers in the area. The Ephraim Bales homestead, for example, is a small cabin set upon rocky land, where the family who lived in the home farmed and from which they made a meager living. The road is also a good starting point for hikes to two of the park's prettiest waterfalls, although finding parking along the narrow road can be tough. The Rainbow Falls Trail begins just after the road becomes one lane and it's only about three miles up a boulder-strewn trail to the seventy-five-foot-tall falls. Farther down the road is the place to start a trek to the twenty-five-foot-high Grotto

Falls, which lies a mile and a half up the Trillium Gap Trail. Near the end of the road there's a wonderful waterfall called "the Place of a Thousand Drips." Drive a little farther, and suddenly you find yourself back in civilization.

Secret Information

Location: Just south of Gatlinburg, down Airport Road (traffic light number 8).
Details: Road closed in winter.

TOP SECRET

If you're lucky, you'll be driving along the Roaring Fork Motor Nature Trail when, suddenly, you'll hear the sound of bluegrass on banjo and guitar coming from in front of the Alfred Reagan Place, home to one of the area's original turn-of-the-century residents, at road marker number 12. On "purty" days between about ten in the morning and six at night, you can see Alfred Reagan's grandson Tolbert and his buddy Otis Benton set up folding chairs just off the road and pick and sing. Eighty-something Tolbert loves to tell stories of growing up along the Roaring Fork, where he lived until he was fourteen. After his wife passed away, he decided to return to his roots and spend his days crooning tunes like "Foggy Mountain Breakdown" for the families that stop to look at his grandfather's "saddlebag" house (two halves around a central chimney) and the small cornmill he built by the creek.

⏹ The Wild Plum Tea Room

Let's Do Lunch

27

We think lunch is a misunderstood meal. These days it too often means stuffing your face with fast food so that you can get back to work as quickly as you can. A midday meal is more of an inconvenience than an experience. It's a strange concept to many that you should actually take some time—right in the middle of the day—to relax some, have a quiet conversation with a friend, savor a carefully prepared sandwich or salad, and maybe even treat yourself to a big gooey dessert.

Well, you can do lunch the way it should be done at the Wild Plum Tea Room. The tiny Austrian-style eatery, open only at midday, is tucked away in a nook just off the Great Smoky Arts and Crafts Community loop (Secret 90) in Gatlinburg, Tennessee. "This place reminds people of why they came to the mountains," manager Cindy Black says. "They can sit by a stream, and it is peaceful and quaint."

Opened in 1985 by Elizabeth and Hubert Hinote, the tiny tea room was named for the wild plum trees outside the old wood and log building standing amid a large stand of trees. A small stream winds its way between the road and the restaurant, creating a barrier to the day's hustle and bustle. Out back, by the kitchen door, is an herb garden that is the source for many of the flavors the restaurant uses in its cuisine.

The inside dining area accommodates just twenty-eight people, although twelve more can sit on the casual screened-in porch in good weather. The main dining room has an Old-World feeling, and the walls are lined with local artists' prints that are for sale.

The menu is short but filled with delicious light dishes like the wild plum medley plate (chicken salad, fresh fruit, and pasta salad) and sandwich and soup choices that change daily. Every table gets a plate of wild plum muffins and almost everyone orders the wild plum tea.

The Wild Plum Tea Room is named for the wild plum trees growing outside. (Photo courtesy of Liz Duckett)

Not so light are the desserts. The most popular, brownie delight, is a chocolate lover's dream of a warm brownie smothered in chocolate sauce and whipped cream. Each day there is a special creation such as coconut cheese cake, hummingbird cake, or sour cream lime pie. Some items, such as the pumpkin pie or amaretto bread, are seasonal. The clientele tend to be couples who return regularly, and the staff go out of their way to make everyone feel unrushed and at home. That's lunch the way it should be.

Secret Information

Location: On the Great Smoky Arts and Crafts Community loop, east of downtown Gatlinburg, Tennessee.

Address: 555 Buckhorn Road, Gatlinburg, Tennessee 37738.

Phone: (423) 436-3808.

Prices: Entrees and sandwiches $6.25 to $6.50; soup $1.95 to $2.95; desserts $2.50 and $3.00.

Hours: 11:30 A.M. to 3:00 P.M., Monday through Saturday, March until mid-December; closed on Thanksgiving Day.

Credit cards: MasterCard, Visa.

Reservations: Recommended.

On the first two weekends of December, the Wild Plum Tea Room hosts lavish holiday feasts like gourmet dinners of crab-stuffed mushrooms, oyster stew, hearts of palm salad, raspberry sorbet, Christmas roast pork, and Christmas cake; or a Williamsburg-style meal with wassail, oysters Rockefeller, King's Arm salad, raspberry sorbet, Smithfield ham, roast Virginia turkey, and Williamsburg date pudding. The cost is about $40 per person; make reservations early.

28

New Age B&B

Plenty of bed-and-breakfasts are tucked away in mountain towns surrounding the Smokies, but we've found only one that doubles as a vegetarian holistic retreat. For some old-fashioned relaxation or some New Age nurturing, stay at Mountain Mist in Waynesville, North Carolina.

Situated in a physician's renovated former home, Mountain Mist sits on the corner of a residential, tree-lined boulevard directly across the street from the lush Waynesville Country Club. The hedge-lined property is filled with wildflowers and huge oak trees, from which several bird feeders are hung. Inside the 1940s rambling brick home, accented with plum wooden shutters, are huge, airy, plush-carpeted bedrooms, each with its own bath, television, VCR, personal telephone, answering machine, and unique style. For example, the back corner room—the Santa Fe—is awash in desert colors and has an iron headboard constructed of horseshoes, while the Captain's Quarters across the hall is decorated in red, white, and blue in a nautical theme.

You can spend a night or two and enjoy a spacious suite, serene setting, and a freshly cooked, meatless breakfast featuring fresh fruit and juices, omelettes, pancakes, cheese, biscuits, cereals, and herbal tea. Or, if you have more time and are looking for a place to "enhance your well-being and your being well," you can enroll in one of the inn's week-long retreat or wellness programs, which include vegetarian dinners. Owners Richard and Joanna Swanson prepare the cuisine and conduct the wellness program, which offers guests a choice of a variety of holistic and New Age options, including "green juice" fasting, nutritional counseling, therapeutic massage, iridology analysis, and something called "colon hydrotherapy" (we're afraid to ask just what that is). You needn't go for all the trendy treatments to spend time feeling better, however. All guests, whether wellness participants or simply bed-and-breakfast folks, can pay extra for massages, facials, and reflexology in the

Even the entrance to the Mountain Mist suggests a cut above the norm.

privacy of their own room. There's also a state-of-the-art exercise room downstairs. It doesn't matter if you're more into the power of pyramids or plain old physical fitness, Mountain Mist offers a healthy dose of Smoky Mountains seclusion.

Secret Information

Location: West end of Waynesville, North Carolina.
Address: 142 Country Club Drive, Waynesville, North Carolina 28786.
Phone: (704) 452-1550.
Rates: $85 to $105 per night for the bed-and-breakfast; $130 to $155 a night or $735 to $1,085 a week for retreat and wellness programs.
Credit cards: MasterCard, Visa.
Details: Children must be nine or older.

TOP SECRET

Even if you're not a golfer, stroll across the street from Mountain Mist to the landmark Waynesville Country Club. Built in 1926, it harks back to an age of elegance when city dwellers sought relief from the heat in the cool North Carolina mountains. In addition to tennis and swimming privileges, Mountain Mist guests can walk the winding golf-cart paths in the early morning before tee time. In the evening treat yourself to dinner in the cozy Tap Room or the locally popular American Heritage Restaurant.

Great Smoky Mountains Railway

All Aboard

29

It takes only twenty minutes to drive from Dillsboro to Bryson City, North Carolina. By train, the same route takes nearly an hour longer. Take the hint. Slow and easy, the pace of the trains that travel the Great Smoky Mountains Railway, is the best way to savor the natural beauty of the southern side of the Smokies.

When starvation nearly set in among the locals in 1846, the decision was made to build a railroad that would link the isolated mountain people of western North Carolina with the outside world. Until 1948 the tracks were the only travel routes around the area for the people of Whittier, Dillsboro, and Bryson City. Contemporary railroad passenger service is strictly for tourists (the line still provides a freight service), although the locals remain very much a part of the railroad. The tracks pass by their front porches and through their strawberry and tobacco fields. Little girls with doll carriages and field laborers handpicking corn stop to smile and wave at the passing passenger cars.

There are six regular daily excursions departing from the completely restored railroad depots in Dillsboro, Bryson City, and Andrews. The shortest regularly scheduled ride is the two-and-a-half-hour Twilight Dinner Train between Dillsboro and Bryson City. The longest is the Nantahala Gorge Raft 'n' Rail run, which includes a seven-mile, guide-assisted raft trip down the raging Nantahala River. In addition, there are several special trips throughout the year, including a murder mystery trip, haunted Halloween trains, and a New Year's Eve gala.

We like the round-trip between Dillsboro and Bryson City because it's the least expensive, yet at three and a half hours it gives the whole family ample time to feel what it's like to ride the rails. The Tuskasegee River run follows the path of the water, providing plenty of chances to see blue heron, beaver, and two-legged tubers and rafters. But the highlight of the trek is the passage through the one-hundred-year-old Cowee Tunnel, which prisoners pick-axed out of

Great Smoky Mountains Railway ■ **69**

All aboard!

The train ride through the Cowee Tunnel means a trip into total darkness. (Lavidge and Associates photo courtesy of Great Smoky Mountains Railway)

the granite mountain. The 186-foot-long tunnel has a sixteen-degree curve, which creates complete darkness for what seems like an eternity. As if that weren't spooky enough, conductor Bill Leonard whispers to all aboard: "Hold your breath all the way through the tunnel so the ghosts won't know you're alive." Apparently, several of the tunnel-construction convicts drowned when their boat capsized on the Tuskasegee, and their bodies are buried on top of the tunnel. Leonard says some passengers swear they see and hear the spirits when they travel through.

Even if you don't see a ghost, you'll probably catch a glimpse of Wild Man, the local character who lives just outside the Cowee Tunnel in a hillside cabin marked by two pink plastic flamingos. Wild Man regularly greets the train with a loud "Hey!" on the way to Bryson City, then showers the folks in the open cars with candy on the way back to Dillsboro.

As the train chugs along, the conductor periodically sounds the whistle, signaling he's about to tell a story about the railway, the river, or the local people. On the Tuskasegee line, the train slows just outside of Dillsboro so everyone can snap a photo of the site where the famous train-wreck scene in the Harrison Ford movie *The Fugitive* was staged. When the train pulls into Bryson City, a bluegrass band greets passengers at the depot with a spirited rendition of *Rocky Top*. Tip: Stay on the same side of the train both coming and going so you won't miss any of the scenery; it'll seem like going on two different train trips.

Secret Information

Location:	Different trips depart from the North Carolina side of the Smokies in Dillsboro, Bryson City, or Andrews.
Address:	P.O. Box 397, Dillsboro, North Carolina 28725-0397.
Phone:	(800) 872-4681.
Web site:	www.gsmr.com.
Hours:	Departure times are from 9:00 A.M. to 7:30 P.M. and vary by time of year and city of departure.
Season:	Late March through December.
Prices:	$18.95 to $52.95 for an adult round-trip ticket; $8.95 to $42.95 for a child's ticket.
Credit cards:	American Express, Discover, MasterCard, Visa.
Reservations:	Accepted.

TOP SECRET

For a memorable ride on the Great Smoky Mountains Railway, pack a picnic lunch and cooler of drinks and purchase tickets to ride in an open-air car. Pulled by diesel engines that run cleaner than steam engines (so there's no soot to get in your eyes or hair), the open-air cars are not only the most inexpensive ride, they also provide unobstructed views, fresh mountain air, and the chance to be the last car on the way out and the first car on the ride back home. If you get too much sun or too cold, you can always take a walk through the silver-colored, covered cars with names like Dixie Flyer, Champion, and Silver Meteor.

Green Mountains

From dark hemlock and rhododendron forests to airy beech tree glades and sweeping heath balds, the Great Smoky Mountains are a unique botanical kingdom of amazingly diverse species of plant life. The variation in greenery is so great because the elevation fluctuates from 857 to 6,643 feet, annual precipitation varies from fifty inches in the lower elevations up to one hundred inches near the summits, and temperatures range from ten to twenty degrees' difference. Such an array of different climates allows plants with widely differing habitat preferences to coexist within a relatively short distance of one another.

Some 6,000 species of plants call the Smokies home, including 130 species of trees, 41 ferns, 300 mosses, 250 lichens, and more than 2,000 fungi. One of more than 1,000 varieties of wildflowers, Rugel's ragwort is found only in the Smokies. There are also at least 17 national-champion trees here, including a 165-foot-tall eastern hemlock that measures almost seventeen feet around its girth and a yellow buckeye with a nineteen-foot waist that stands 136 feet tall. Old-growth trees are the exception, however. When the Great Smoky Mountains National Park was established in the 1930s, 60 percent of its area had already been logged over, so the second-growth forest is a mere fifty or sixty years old.

There are a dozen or so distinct forest types, all scattered about in broad patches. In the beautiful cove hardwoods, found below 4,500 feet, eastern hemlock, Carolina silverbell, yellow buckeye, beetree linden (white basswood), sugar maple, and yellow birch predominate. Also present are smatterings of many other species and a verdant carpet of ferns and other herbaceous plants beneath. Red oak-hickory forests occur usually below 2,500 to 3,000 feet. Concentrations of hemlock form dense forests of large trees at various elevations. The gray beech forest has small trees and occurs above 4,500 feet.

Above 5,500 feet, spruce-fir forests used to dominate much of the

Here are a few of the trees in the Smokies that survived loggers decades earlier. (Photo courtesy of Great Smoky Mountains National Park)

park's northeast terrain. Now, however, the firs have been nearly all destroyed by the balsam woolly adelgid, a sucking insect. All that is left are naked, dead spires. Although all of the mature Fraser firs have been lost, there are small clusters of seedlings growing. The balsam woolly adelgid attacks only mature trees, and there is hope that some of these young ones—and if they live long enough to bear progeny, their young—will show a natural resistance to the insects.

Many people trek to the Smokies only for the flowers. From mid-April to mid-May, the Smokies burst with spring wildflowers—trillium, Dutchman's breeches, toothwort, umbrella leaf, trout lily, columbine, foamflower, and others. From mid-June to mid-July, rhododendrons, azaleas, and mountain laurel—all members of the heath family—are in glorious bloom, depending on location. The rose-purple flowers of the Catawba rhododendron, sometimes interspersed with mountain laurel, are easily seen by car and by foot. Also ablaze with color are the heath balds—so called because the azaleas, rhododendron, and mountain laurel dominate the landscape. Park rangers frequently conduct hikes to see them.

Secret Information

For more information about Smoky Mountains flora, check out *Wildflowers of the Smokies* by biology professor and arboretum director Peter White and others (Great Smoky Mountains Natural History Association, 1996); *Great Smoky Mountains Wildflowers* by Robert W. Hutson, William F. Hutson, and Aaron J. Sharp (Windy Pines Publishing, 1995); and *Wildlife Watcher's Guide: Great Smoky Mountains National Park* by Mike Carlton (North Wood Press, Inc.).

TOP SECRET

Although more than half of the Great Smoky Mountains National Park has been logged, it's still home to patches of primordial old-growth forests and some record-size trees. One of the best places to view virgin forest is along Albright Grove Loop Trail, a circle off the Maddron Bald Trail, which starts off U.S. Highway 321 near Cosby, Tennessee. The oldest known tree is a 564-year-old black gum tree on the Greenbrier Pinnacle near Pittman Center. The tree with the largest diameter is a tulip poplar near Greenbrier Ridge, midway between Tremont and Elkmont, that is twenty-four feet around. The tallest tree is a white pine, which stands 187 feet tall near Booger Man Trail in Cataloochee at the east end of the park. For those who are more interested in beauty than age, one of the best places to see wildflowers is the Porter's Creek Trail, which starts near the Greenbrier entrance to the park off U.S. Highway 321.

31

Water World

East Tennesseans love their lakes. Thanks to the Tennessee Valley Authority, which in the 1930s and 1940s created a series of man-made lakes and dams in the region for flood control and hydroelectric power, the area is flush with wide, mild lakes perfect for fishing, boating, swimming, and jet and water skiing.

The closest TVA lake to the Tennessee side of the Smokies is Douglas. With its 30,400 acres of water surface, Douglas is one big lake. And although it's only eight miles north of Sevierville, Douglas is a world away from the neon nightmare stretch between that town and Pigeon Forge. With fifty-four miles of shoreline, the lake is serene, clean, and the ideal spot to forget the world for a while and just float.

Those with a boat or other watercraft in tow should head to the many marinas and ramps that offer places to put in, especially around Douglas Dam. For those of us who don't own a watercraft, however, the place to spend the day on the water is Swann's Marina in Dandridge. There Smoky Mountains visitors can rent boats, buy bait and tackle, and even rent a campsite or a bare-bones one- to three-room fishing cabin (beds, kitchenette, utensils, dishes—bring your own bath and kitchen towels and soap) for the night or week.

The folks at Swann's, situated on Swann's Point just up from Swann Road (as you can tell, the Swanns were a prominent local family in the early days of Dandridge), can make any flatland land-lubber the captain of his or her own lake-faring vessel. The marina rents aluminum or fiberglass fishing boats with six-horsepower motors and twenty-four-foot homemade float boats—basically a flat boat with a picnic table anchored on board—with forty-horsepower motors. Your best bet for fun and comfort, however, is the twenty-two-foot crest pontoon boat with a retractable roof, padded seats, a dining area, and a forty-horsepower motor.

Pack a cooler with drinks, a picnic basket with munchies, and if you forget anything, the little store at Swann's Marina probably has what you're looking for. The crew at Swann's—ask for Bobby Murph, he's been there "forever," he says—will gas you up, give you enough instructions to feel comfortable, fit everyone with a life jacket, then direct you to the prettiest parts of the lake.

Besides great views, dozens of small islands dot Douglas, creating plenty of secret coves where boaters can stop, shut down the motor, and spend awhile swimming off the back deck or reading, sunbathing, or picnicking on board. Bring your binoculars and you might spot a bald eagle along with the hawks and herons native to Douglas.

Swann's will rent boats by the hour, for six hours, the day (eight hours), or for twenty-four hours. We suggest you set aside a day to get the full flavor of the lake. When you do finally (and reluctantly) make it back to the marina, the crew will guide you in and fill the gas tank back up (you pay for only the gas you use).

Secret Information

Location: Swann's Marina is just off I-40 (exit 432) in Tennessee.
Address: 2515 Swann's Marina Road, Dandridge, Tennessee 37725-9401.
Phone: (423) 397-2182.
Prices: Fishing boat $35 per day; float boat $80 per day; pontoon boat $120 a day.
Credit cards: MasterCard, Visa.
Details: A $200 security deposit (credit cards accepted) is required on all boat rentals. Life jackets are required and can be rented for $1 each. A maximum of ten passengers can ride on both the float and pontoon boats. Boats must be rented for a minimum of two hours. Booking in advance is suggested and a $50 deposit (credit cards accepted) is required, although during the week you can probably rent a boat without a reservation.

TOP SECRET

If touring Douglas Lake on a personal watercraft (such as a jet ski or wave-runner) is more your style than boating, head to Swann's Marina, but don't walk out on the dock. Instead, visit the wooden gazebo at the head of the ramp. This is the open-air office of H_2O Sports, which rents one-, two-, and three-seater personal watercraft for $45 an hour. For more information, call 888-WET-JETS (938-5387).

32

On Top of Old Smoky

Even if the Von Bryan Inn isn't the highest bed-and-breakfast in the Smokies (in terms of altitude), we bet it has the best view. Situated atop a twenty-one-hundred-foot-high mountain, the six-room main house commands a 360-degree vista of the lush green Wears Valley, Tennessee, with the peaks of the Great Smoky Mountains National Park on one side and the sweeping Tennessee Valley on the other.

"We've had guests who have sat on our front porch and seen Mount LeConte," proprietor Jo Ann Vaughn says, "and others who have climbed Mount LeConte have seen our place from out on Myrtle's Point. We really are at the top of the world."

The man who originally cleared the oak trees off the pinnacle of Hatcher Mountain to build a personal vacation retreat died before his dream was realized. Along came Jo Ann and her husband, D. J., who bought the unfinished log home shell and realized a dream by opening a mountaintop bed-and-breakfast.

"The neighbors were real curious when we first purchased the property," says Jo Ann, who, with the help of her husband and grown sons, David and Patrick, lovingly landscaped and completed the elegant sixty-one-hundred-foot-plus, two-story log inn. "Apparently, the previous owners' dogs had never let anyone come close to the house, so no one knew what was going on up here. They did know about the trees being taken down, however, and they weren't happy about that."

When the Vaughns (the name of the inn is a combination of their surname abbreviated and that of one the area's earliest settlers, the Bryans) moved in, they welcomed their new neighbors to the previously unseen dwelling. Finally, everyone saw how cutting down some of the oak trees wasn't such a bad idea. The view from the mountaintop inn now attracts visitors from around the globe—including one Zimbabwean statesman who invited the innkeepers to go

The view from the Von Bryan Inn is almost "top of the world." (Photo courtesy of the Von Bryan Inn)

elephant hunting. And from the surrounding woods, fox, wild turkey, hawks, bluebirds, and goldfinches have shared the inn's lush front lawn with the Vaughns' lovable collie, Little Man.

"I'd say most guests come back for the view and the food," says Jo Ann, whose scrumptious desserts (left out for late-night munchers) are just one of the reasons the inn was only one of twenty-five in the nation to earn the prestigious America's Favorite Inns Award in 1997. "Once people get here they have a hard time coming up with a reason to leave."

The winding ten-minute, two-and-a-half-mile drive leading up to the inn might also help convince guests to stay put and savor either Jo Ann's bountiful breakfast buffet or a good book in front of the massive stacked-stone fireplace in the vaulted-ceiling living room. Snuggling under comfy quilts, hand-stitched by Jo Ann's mom, or rocking away the day on one of the covered front porches or on the sprawling deck near the glimmering swimming pool and hot tub, isn't such a bad way to pass a day either.

Inside, the Von Bryan Inn is both grandiose and cozy. (Photo courtesy of the Von Bryan Inn)

Secret Information

Location: Off Highway 321, in Wears Valley near Pigeon Forge, Tennessee.

Address: 2402 Hatcher Mountain Road, Sevierville, Tennessee 37862.

Phone: (800) 633-1459 or (423) 453-9832.

Fax: (423) 428-8634.

E-mail: von-bryan-inn@juno.com.

Web site: www.bbonline.com/tn/vonbryan.

Rates: $90 to $135 for rooms in the inn and $180 per night (two-night minimum) for up to four people in the log chalet.

Season: Year-round.

Credit cards: American Express, Discover, MasterCard, Visa.

TOP SECRET

The newest addition to the Von Bryan Inn is the open and airy Sugar Maple Room situated on the front end of the original structure. Perfect for two, it offers panoramic views of the valley from its private corner porch and features a sharply slanted wooden ceiling and a unique three-tier ceiling over the whirlpool bath that resembles a massive wedding cake.

Kids Camps in the Smokies

Camp Smoky

33

Summer camp is a rite of passage for kids. For many it's the first time away from Mom and Dad for any length of time. It's also a chance to have a blast with newfound friends met hiking, swimming, singing around a campfire, making crafts, eating strange-looking food, or enjoying all the other rituals of a week or two away in the woods.

Few summer camps are as special for kids as those offered by the Great Smoky Mountains Institute at Tremont inside the national park. That's because the children who come to camp in the mountains every year from all over the eastern United States also get fascinating first-hand lessons in conservation and ecology.

The institute, established in 1969 by area naturalists, describes itself as a great way "to connect people with nature" through different levels of year-round environmental and educational programs in the heart of southern Appalachia. It's operated by the Great Smoky Mountains Natural History Association, a private, nonprofit organization; and it hosts two camp programs for kids of different ages.

The first is Discovery Camp, which lasts one week in July. The nine- to twelve-year-olds who attend stay in a large 125-bed dormitory (girls on one side, boys on the other) at Tremont near Cades Cove in Tennessee. They are divided into "family groups," who make collective decisions on how to spend time. As a group, they perform such activities as animal tracking, making a fire without matches, weaving baskets and dream catchers, and wading through creeks to study the creepie crawlies that live there. The twelve-year-olds also go on an overnight trip as an introduction to backpacking. Arts and crafts include a game called "float it," in which a child makes a boat out of materials such as leaves and nutshells. Kids also get personal time, when they can do such things as write about nature in journals or sketch the landscape. "The beauty of this Discovery Camp is that education just creeps up on kids. If you told them they were going to science class, they wouldn't want to go," says Kathy Burns, who works at the Institute.

During Wilderness Camp, which is held three weeks a year, thirteen- to seventeen-year-olds actually get into the mountain wilderness and develop outdoor skills. Such activities include ridge climbing, exploration of old-growth forests, swimming in mountain streams, storytelling around a backcountry campfire, hiking at night, and canoeing. Campers are also taught park-resource management, not only by expert naturalists but also through hands-on experience. They actually visit a black bear den site, track red wolves, and learn about backcountry campsite management and water-quality management. Such experiences create a sense of camaraderie and teach cooperation skills. Many participants end up considering a career with the park service.

Secret Information

Location: Kids camps are held at the Great Smoky Mountains Institute in the Tremont area of the Great Smoky Mountains National Park.

Address: Great Smoky Mountains Institute at Tremont, 9275 Tremont Road, Townsend, Tennessee 37882.

Phone: (423) 448-6709.

Fax: (423) 448-9250.

E-mail: gsmit@smoky.igc.apc.org.

Rates: Discovery Camp $210; Wilderness Camp $270 (minimum deposit of $50 for either camp).

Credit cards: American Express, Discover, MasterCard, Visa.

TOP SECRET

Kids don't have to spend a week at summer camp in the Smokies to have fun exploring the national park's flora and fauna. During the tourist season, park rangers lead a variety of free educational programs that appeal to the pint-sized set. Every day from June through August, for example, there are Junior Ranger programs conducted at Cades Cove, Cosby, Elkmont, and Smokemont campgrounds. Kids receive a workbook outlining several activities they must complete, such as picking up trash, attending a ranger talk, and taking a nature hike. Those who successfully fulfill the requirements, which can be accomplished in one day, are awarded plastic Junior Ranger badges and special certificates at an afternoon award ceremony at the Sugarlands Visitor Center. For more information on what's happening for kids in the Smokies, stop at any of the park's visitor centers or call (423) 436-1200.

Breakfast at Its Best

34

There are plenty of places to eat breakfast in Maggie Valley, North Carolina. But *the* place to eat is Joey's. The line winding out the door around the antique horse wagon gives it away. People would rather wait to eat at Joey's than ride down the road and sit right down. Perhaps this is because Joey's specializes in morning meals. The place is open only from 7:00 A.M. until noon, and it's usually packed the entire time.

The secret of the restaurant's success is Joey and Brenda O'Keefe, who've owned the operation since 1966. A warm and welcoming woman, Brenda buzzes among the tables greeting old friends and visitors with the same broad smile. Her personal touch extends even to the two-pound bags of Joey's secret golden pancake mix sold in the restaurant gift shop for $5.50. "100% natural—brought to you with love by Brenda," reads a handwritten note on every label. Even if the batter mixes up real well back home, there is no way it can match actually sitting down at Joey's under the massive wagon-wheel light fixtures suspended from the sloping ceiling and diving into an order of the mountain blueberry pancakes or the sausage roll-up (pure pork sausage rolled in two fluffy cakes).

The wooden tables and chairs are crammed together to ensure there's always room for one more. You can't help but feel at home when the party next to you is close enough to pass bottles of syrup or an extra dollop of butter. To help keep the country cousin closeness from becoming claustrophobic, however, the restaurant walls are mainly windowed—offering lush views of the nearby mountain ridges as well as passersby on busy Soco Road.

Joey's gets its share of tourists, even without advertising in any of the local vacationer publications. The locals patiently wait for a table with the crowd and no one pressures anyone to eat and run. Servers gladly keep the bottomless cups of coffee filled and offer friendly advice on what's best on the menu—basically anything with a pancake.

There's always room for one more at Joey's Pancake House.

The kids' choices are varied and include a drink for about three dollars or under. Although the three small pancakes and egg or bacon is probably the best deal for the small fries, the happy face pancake—decorated with whipped cream and chocolate chips—is our daughters' favorite. There are also heart-healthy items such as slow-cooked oatmeal and fresh-fruit plates and Belgian waffles. Mom always said breakfast is the most important meal of the day; she'll get no argument from us as long as we can eat it at Joey's.

Secret Information

Location: On U.S. Highway 19, in Maggie Valley, North Carolina.
Address: P.O. Box 298, Maggie Valley, North Carolina 28751.
Phone: (704) 926-1678 or (704) 926-0212.
Hours: 7:00 A.M. until noon daily.
Prices: Breakfasts $2.98–$5.99.
Credit cards: MasterCard, Visa.

TOP SECRET

Check out the huge sixty-four-square quilt hanging on the wall above the grill at Joey's Pancake House. The squares are actually T-shirts collected by Maggie Valley's first mayor, Woody Fowler, from various biking and running races he competed in over the years. There are a few from the town's own annual Maggie Valley Moonlight Race and even one from the 1985 Boston Marathon. Fowler is a longtime patron of the pancake house and a friend of the O'Keefes. He sent off the T-shirts to a company that turns personal items into quilts, and then he presented it to Joey and Brenda O'Keefe as a gift.

Going Underground

The Smokies are riddled with mazes of caves, but you'd have to be a serious spelunker to explore most of them. Not so at the ominous-sounding Forbidden Caverns. It can't compare, of course, to Mammoth Cave or Carlsbad Caverns; but if you're looking for a unique perspective on the Smokies, go underground.

Forbidden Caverns offers a light show that tells the tale of an Indian princess and the forbidden hollow mountain, but the presentation isn't hokey enough to detract from the real star of this show—the living cave with its growing stalagmites, stalactites, flow stones, and onyx formations.

The caverns are situated in a secluded valley near Sevierville, Tennessee, dotted with rustic barns and cabins and rolling hills. Some believe that the river running through the cave comes from a secret lake hidden under English Mountain, but no one knows for sure. The water leaves the cave at a crack in the rocks and reappears down the road at the now-closed English Mountain Trout Farm. Although trout obviously survived in that portion of the river, the underground part is fish free because it's 99 percent pure water and contains nothing for aqua life to eat.

The caverns weave under English Mountain and have provided shelter for both Native Americans and moonshiners. Arrowheads have been recovered from the cave; and the remnants of a moonshine still, which was destroyed by federal agents in 1948, remain as part of the tour. The guide's monologue, peppered with down-home jokes and local lore, provides a brief overview of how rock formations live and die, but the greatest lessons are gained simply by slowly walking through the narrow rock passages and looking up, down, and all around.

Other commercial caves have paved walkways, more akin to a cave mall than a natural wonder, but Forbidden Caverns is simple, rustic (except for the iron handrails), and awesome all on its own. There's the largest formation of rare cave onyx in the nation, at 175 feet tall and 105 feet wide; spacious grottoes with landscapes reminiscent of the desert Southwest or the moon; and towering natural chimneys. The owners (a group of local businessmen) even preserved the cave's natural entrance, through which sunlight and rain stream down three hundred feet to the cave floor.

The cave is a cool oasis on a hot summer day; even if it's sweltering outside, bring a jacket or sweatshirt on your trek. The guided tours, which leave as often as a group of ten or so assembles in the gift shop, are approximately fifty-five minutes long. At a constant temperature of fifty-eight degrees, the underground tour can start to feel a bit nippy, especially if you're wearing short sleeves.

Secret Information

Location: Off U.S. Highway 411, between Sevierville and Newport, Tennessee.
Address: 455 Blowing Cave Road, Sevierville, Tennessee 37876.
Phone: (423) 453-5972.
Prices: Adults $8; children $4.
Hours: 9:00 A.M. to 6:00 P.M., from June to August; 10:00 A.M. to 5:00 P.M., in April, May, September, October, and early November.

TOP SECRET

If you are a serious and experienced spelunker planning a vacation in the Smokies and would like to hook up with a local grotto (caver talk for *chapter*), there are two active area groups you can write to arrange to see the less-accessible underbelly of the Smokies. They are the Smoky Mountain Grotto (Box 8297, UT Station, Knoxville, Tennessee 37996) and the East Tennessee Grotto (320 Wardley Road, Knoxville, Tennessee 37922-1829). For online info on Tennessee caving, cave safety and conservation, links to other caving sites, and pictures of caves in the Southeast, visit the Upper Cumberland Grotto Home Cave at www.tntechedu/www/life/orgs/index.html.

36

I Scream for Ice Cream

The problem with America is that there no longer are any good places to get sarsaparilla. We think that the decline of this country's culture can be directly traced to the disappearance of soda fountains, where you can sit at the counter and suck down handmade malted milk shakes, cherry cokes, and strawberry sodas. The classic ice cream parlor is a symbol of simpler times—of sharing a chocolate soda (two straws, please) with your best guy or girl, of talking about the big game over a big brown cow, of getting high on sugar and nothing else.

A bit of that idealized past is preserved at the Soda Fountain in a small mall in the Great Smoky Arts and Crafts Community (Secret 90) near Gatlinburg, Tennessee, Larry Albritton, who also owns the mall's Apple Annie's shop, re-created the old-time snack shop with the intent of serving every kind of traditional treat you can remember.

Patrons entering the Soda Fountain can hear World War II–era music emanating from an old floor-standing radio. Sit down at the small counter on red-seated stools or choose a chair at one of the handful of tables. The walls are covered with Coke signs from the thirties and forties. There are Coke clocks, model Old Ice Cream and Hershey's trucks, soda fountain mugs, prints of old soda fountain stores, old-photograph magnets, old-style Coke advertising card decks, and other memorabilia for sale. The atmosphere strives to be as authentic as possible—the soda taps were built in 1932 and 1937, and the cash register is a genuine monster from 1923.

The menu also is a blast from the past, featuring cones, shakes, sodas, flavored Cokes, and, yes, even sarsaparilla. A true soda jerk makes everything from scratch—the syrup and carbonated water to make a Coke is even mixed directly in the glass rather than by a machine. Small touches such as serving the leftovers in the steel mixing tumbler with a milk shake are the norm. Choices that you can't find in the average Baskin-Robbins include lime phosphates and other flavors mixed in carbonated water. Snack items like nachos, big and warm pretzels, hot dogs, cookies, and brownies, as well as coffee, cappuccino, and espresso fill out the fattening fare. Bowing a bit to modern times, however, the menu also features fat-free and sugar-free ice creams and frozen yogurts.

Albritton recently sold the Soda Fountain and now serves as a consultant to owner Sandy Ryalls. Albritton is franchising the Soda Fountain concept. A similar store has opened along the main strip in Gatlinburg, and he hopes to spread them to tourist areas throughout the United States and around the globe. Maybe the world will be a better place with a few more old-fashioned ice cream parlors in it.

Secret Information

Location: On the Great Smoky Arts and Crafts Community loop, east of downtown Gatlinburg, Tennessee.
Address: 601 Glades Road, Suite #20, Gatlinburg, Tennessee 37738.
Phone: (423) 430-7881.
Hours: 10:00 A.M. to 5:30 P.M. daily.
Prices: 75¢ to $4.
Credit cards: Discover, MasterCard, Visa.

TOP SECRET

The Soda Fountain is the only place in the Smokies we know where you can get an authentic egg cream. No, there's no egg in it, or even cream. It's just a mixture of chocolate syrup and soda water—an ice cream soda without the ice cream. Few tourists from the South are familiar with the concoction, says one of the shop's staff, "but we have to have egg creams on the menu for the New Yorkers."

Balsam Mountain Campground

37 Cool Camping

The Balsam Mountain Campground is known as the coolest campsite in the Great Smoky Mountains National Park. That's cool on two counts.

First, the temperature, a mile above sea level, is a good twenty degrees cooler than it is down in the flatland. Rangers call it "the air-conditioned campground" because it's the best place in the park to pitch a tent and beat the heat during the hot sweaty dog days of July and August. Unlike some of the other campsites in the park that can be reserved, Balsam operates on a self-service, first-come, first-served system. Be sure to check at either the Sugarlands Visitor Center in Tennessee or the Oconaluftee Visitor Center in North Carolina to see if there are sites available before you make the trek up the crest of Balsam Mountain on the southeastern side of the national park.

Second, the mountaintop location—the highest campground in the park at 5,310 feet—is miles from any tourists or tubers and is an awesome home base for some serious hiking and backcountry exploration. Even for those who aren't hard-core outdoorspeople, there are attractions like the spectacular 5,327-foot Heintooga Overlook. There's also a good chance that you'll see black bear while staying in the Balsam Mountain area (whether you think that's good or bad is up to you). The area's abundance of blackberries, herbs, and beetles in the cool, wet atmosphere tends to draw the park's famous furry residents. To help campers keep their bear neighbors safe, rangers regularly offer a weekend presentation "A Fed Bear Is a Dead Bear" at the Balsam Mountain campfire circle. Many bears each year are hit by cars because some people feed them from their vehicles. Also, bears that learn to subsist on cookies and hot dogs don't do so well when they have to forage for food in the wild. To reach the circle, walk down the campground road to the end, then follow the wooded path for sixty yards. Even if there's no ranger program going on, the circle is the ideal spot to meet fellow outdoor enthusiasts, stargaze, and invent ways to tell the folks back home that you've found heaven and aren't coming back.

Secret Information

Location: On the southeast border of the Great Smoky Mountains National Park, east of Cherokee, North Carolina.

Prices: $10 to $12 per site.

Campsites: 46; maximum vehicle size, 30 feet.

Season: May through September.

For more information call (423) 436-1230.

38

Moot Music

Waynesville, North Carolina, is one of the last places on earth you would expect to meet dancers from Sierra Leone or singers from Slovenia. Folks who live in these parts know better. For ten days each July, the traditionally sleepy Smoky Mountains town just off the Blue Ridge Parkway is transformed into a mini-United Nations of sorts. That's when Waynesville welcomes the world via Folkmoot U.S.A., an annual festival featuring a dozen or so traditional music and dance troupes from around the globe.

The idea for the cultural celebration, held since 1984, came from Waynesville resident Dr. Clinton Barker, a well-traveled guy who thought the Smoky Mountains setting back home would be the perfect site for a folk festival similar to the ones he had enjoyed overseas. In fact, Folkmoot—an Old English word meaning "meeting of the people"—is the name of the annual bash held in Newcastle upon Tyne in England.

Although the concept and the performers have foreign roots, the flavor of Folkmoot U.S.A. is pure southern Appalachian. More than six hundred local folks volunteer to handle all the backstage tasks, downtown decoration, cleanup, and cooking. Area schools are converted into temporary hostels to house the visitors. Throughout the festival, traditional Appalachian music and dance are performed by area troupes as the official American ingredient in this lively multicultural mix. On opening day, usually a Friday night in mid-July, the Folkmoot U.S.A. performers parade down Main Street in all their traditional finery. Tourists and home folks line sidewalks decorated with the flags of each participating country. Before the nighttime performance at nearby Maggie Valley, the international performers, guests, and locals mingle and swap howdies on the lawn in front of Waynesville's courthouse.

Folkmoot U.S.A. turns Waynesville, North Carolina, into a mini-United Nations each July. (Johnny Cope photo)

There are daily performances throughout the Waynesville–Maggie Valley area. Some events are free and others require tickets. There is also a full slate of cultural-education classes held around the region in conjunction with Folkmoot U.S.A. Both children and adults can take part in traditional dance and music courses at area schools. They can also participate in lively discussions on current events and international culture with the visiting performers.

Groups can only perform at Folkmoot U.S.A. one time, so if you attend one year, you'll enjoy a completely different slate of acts the next. This once-in-a-lifetime attitude permeates the festival and makes every performance an emotionally charged event. Many of these groups have scrimped and saved for years to earn the plane fare to the United States for this festival, and they take great pride in finally getting the opportunity to represent their native country. None of these singers or dancers are professional performers. All work for a living in various careers ranging from farming to teaching to engineering, so when they get their shot in the spotlight at Folkmoot U.S.A., they give it all they've got.

Appalachian music and dance are celebrated throughout the Folkmoot festival. (Johnny Cope photo)

Secret Information

Location: Folkmoot events take place at various locations throughout the Waynesville–Maggie Valley area of North Carolina, including a candlelight closing ceremony at Lake Junaluska. The opening parade and International Festival Day both take place in downtown Waynesville.

Address: P.O. Box 658, Waynesville, North Carolina 28786.

Phone: (704) 452-2997.

Prices: Tickets are $13 for performances featuring all of the groups and $8 for shows where only three groups perform. Children's performances are $3; no reserved seating is available. There are also free performances. Reserved seats for non-children's performances go on sale May 1.

Schedule: Folkmoot U.S.A. occurs over ten days starting in mid-July and ends on the last Sunday of the month.

TOP SECRET

If you can pick only one day to devote to Folkmoot U.S.A., make it International Festival Day, usually held the second Saturday of the event. Waynesville's population of sixty-eight hundred roughly triples on this day, making the event the largest of the year in Haywood County. The numbers are spread among more than one hundred booths featuring international food and crafts, as well as on-street pavilions for music and dance. While sampling some tasty international treats, you'll also have a chance to talk with the performers, who spend the day walking among the people at the miniworld bazaar set up downtown.

Wedding Daze

"Couples meet on Friday night, drive to the Smokies on Saturday, find out they can't get a license on Sunday, and get married on Monday," says Reverend Jerry McClelland, the pastor who presides over as many as thirty wedding ceremonies a day at the Chapel by the Courthouse in downtown Sevierville, Tennessee. "Then about two days later they wake up and wonder what they've done."

All told, eighteen thousand or so couples get married in Sevier County each year, making the county, which includes Pigeon Forge and Gatlinburg, the Las Vegas of the South. It's the place to head to when you can't wait another minute to make your love legal. There's no waiting period for a marriage license in Tennessee. All you need to get one is proof of age—no blood test is required. It's harder to get a driver's license here than to commit to someone 'til death do you part.

Thanks to this marriage-made-easy system and the popularity of the Smokies as a honeymoon destination, a booming business of throwing turnkey weddings has sprung up in Sevier and surrounding counties. Some couples stop by the Sevier County Courthouse—a gold-domed building with a statue of Dolly Parton out front—for a license, then step across the street to McClelland and wedding planner Lana Turner's storefront that displays fourteen neon hearts in the window. Couples pay forty-nine dollars and up to say, "I do," sometimes clad only in T-shirts and shorts. Others opt for one of the dozens of other fancier commercial chapels in the area. Places like Cupid's Chapel of Love in Gatlinburg promote storybook ceremonies staged inside quaint country churchlike buildings or outside in gazebos as part of packages that can include anything a bride and groom could want: flowers, photos, videos, music, a cake, a limousine, a reception for dozens of guests, honeymoon arrangements, and even a ceremony in a helicopter. Such nuptials range in price from a couple hundred dollars to several thousand. The most popular time to

A little touch of snow is never enough to keep loving couples from tying the knot at Cupid's Chapel of Love, in Gatlinburg. (Photo courtesy of Cupid's Chapel of Love, Gatlinburg, Tennessee)

get married in the Smokies is on Valentine's Day and during May, June, and October.

Unfortunately, weddings are such big business that some of the chapels have a bit of a drive-through feel to them. Of course, the chapels are in it for profit, so there's likely to be some pressure applied to buy the most expensive packages. Ministers also vary in the amount of religious preaching they do in their ceremonies: Remember, this is the Bible Belt. Our advice is to take the time to check out the competition before you settle on a chapel. This is to make sure you're getting the best deal and that your wedding won't feel rushed, impersonal, or nonreflective of your faith.

If you want to take the time and trouble to have a do-it-yourself wedding with the real romance of nature all around you, you can choose to say your vows inside the Great Smoky Mountains National Park proper. You can get hitched anywhere there—on top of Mount LeConte, inside a primitive church in Cades Cove, or beside Abrams Falls—for free, but you have to get a permit in advance, hire your own minister or other presiding official, and obey various rules to prevent damage to the park and to avoid disturbing other visitors.

Secret Information

To get a marriage license in Sevier County, head to the county court clerk's office in the courthouse in downtown Sevierville. The office is open from 8:00 A.M. to 4:30 P.M., Monday through Friday, and from 8:00 A.M. to 11:00 P.M. on Saturday. There is also a satellite office in Gatlinburg on Reagan Drive (open 8:30 A.M. to 4:00 P.M., Monday, Tuesday, Thursday, and Friday; 8:30 A.M. to 12:00 P.M. on Wednesday; and 9:00 A.M. to 3:00 P.M. on Saturday) and at the Pigeon Forge City Hall on Pine Mountain Road (open Saturday from 9:00 A.M. to 5:00 P.M.). Licenses are $36 and all you need to get one is proof of age (a birth certificate or driver's license). No waiting period or blood test is required. To get married in the Great Smoky Mountains National Park, apply for a permit at least a month in advance. Call (423) 436-1200 for rules and restrictions.

TOP SECRET

Folks have been flocking to Temple Feed, Seed, and Fertilizer across the street from the Sevier County Courthouse since 1916 for farm supplies and quick weddings. Although the aisles of pet food, fertilizer, and rodent killer and the smell of rawhide dog treats and sawdust can't compare with the crushed-velvet trappings and floral scents of local wedding chapels, thousands of couples have been married over the years by store owner and justice of the peace James A. Temple, who considers pronouncing a couple man and wife his civic duty and doesn't charge anything for the service. He surely wouldn't object if you bought a few bales of hay off the loading dock, however, for the honeymoon. For more information on arranging a feed and seed union, call Temple at (423) 453-3341.

40 A Novel Destination

Time Capsule Books is one of those places you probably wouldn't stumble across unless you got lost. It's housed in a two-story, pale yellow bungalow that's more than a century old and tucked in a grove of towering pines. Bill Lee, a former newspaperman, figures he gets about five out of every hundred visitors who are lucky enough to find the quaint mountain village of Dillsboro, North Carolina, about thirty miles south of the Great Smoky Mountains National Park. Those averages wouldn't be good for most businesses, but they're just fine with Lee.

"I don't get the cotton-candy-fingered crowd," he says as he prepares to eat lunch at his worn wooden desk surrounded by shelves of first editions, leather-bound and signed books, and extensive collections of North Carolina and southern fiction. "I get the people who stay in the bed-and-breakfasts instead of the motels. I get the people who love books."

Time Capsule is a book lover's vacation destination. The little house with creaky narrow staircase and eclectic mix of oriental rugs and carpeting is a comfortable, welcoming place to spend an afternoon browsing through Civil War histories or mysteries or regional books about the Appalachians. There are more than ten thousand titles to choose from, including used, out-of-print, and rare volumes. (Feel free to bring along a few books to trade.) The sounds of classical music are periodically muffled by the whistle and steam of the Great Smoky Mountains Railway train (Secret 29), passing mere yards from the store.

Beside Lee's desk is a straight-backed wooden chair worn in the seat where visitors have stopped to sit a spell and chat. Lee encourages everyone who comes in to pull up the chair and share stories. Over the years he's had guests from England, France, and every state—collectors of first editions, history buffs, and Appalachian-culture aficionados. Adds Lee, who was forty-six when he left

Time Capsule Books is tucked away in a grove of towering pines, offering the perfect setting for avid book readers who love a good page turner.

newspapers to become proprietor, "Every day I'm here I meet someone new with some fascinating story to tell."

Secret Information

Location: Just across the railroad tracks and up the hill from downtown Dillsboro, North Carolina.

Address: 10 Craft Circle, Dillsboro, North Carolina 28725.

Phone: (704) 586-1026.

Hours: 10:00 A.M. to 5:30 P.M., Monday through Saturday; 1:00 P.M. to 4:00 P.M., Sunday during the summer.

Credit cards: MasterCard, Visa.

TOP SECRET

Time Capsule Books owner Bill Lee is an expert on North Carolina and the author of *A Newcomer's Guide to North Carolina* (1996, Down Home Press, $14.95). On page one he mentions the state motto, *"Esse Quam Videre,"* which he tells us means "To be, rather than to seem." That motto describes Lee to a T, literally: Stop by his store and he'll tell you anything you ever wanted to know about the Tar Heel state.

41

Bald Spots

As early as 1800, explorers and naturalists reported that some mountaintops in the Smokies bore windswept, treeless, grassy crowns—even though the tallest one is surrounded by higher, fully forested peaks. Eight balds in the Smokies have been given names—Andrews Bald, Double Springs Gap, Gregory Bald, Little Bald, Parson Bald, Russell Field, Silers Bald, and Spence Field. Yet the question of how these strange treeless areas came to be has never been answered. Are they natural or man-made?

Some scientists have speculated that lightning, climatic extremes, windfall, and landslides might have decimated trees there. Then new seedlings could not gain a foothold once the mountain oat grass became a dominant species, and the balds became summer pastures for livestock. Valley settlers valued the areas because the grass was rich and the climate cool. Also they didn't have to fence their animals out of field and vegetable crops.

Every spring, as soon as the weather warmed, word spread that the local herders were ready to move the animals up the mountain to the strange open places. Families from as far away as sixty miles contributed livestock—usually some ten to twenty cows and fifteen to twenty sheep—and paid roughly a dollar a head for cattle, a quarter for each sheep, and a couple bucks each for horses and mules so that a herder could tend them all summer. Soil compaction and heavy grazing could have certainly played a part in keeping these balds clear. Despite the once-popular notion that they are stable and permanent, balds actually need selective applications of herbicides and controlled burns every few years to keep them free of trees.

Grazing, however, doesn't completely explain why the balds exist. The heath balds, so called because the dominant plants—azaleas, rhododendrons, mountain laurel, and blueberries, among others—are all members of the heath family, were never used for feeding livestock.

How these areas evolved is a mystery. It's possible that a natural event—a storm, fire, or landslide, for example—cleared an area near which these heath shrubs already were growing. Their dense growth and the fact that they increase soil acidity probably prevented trees from gaining a foothold.

Regardless of how they were formed, the balds, with their unobstructed views and colorful shrubbery, are some of the most beautiful places to hike to in the park. When the heath balds come into bloom, mountaintops are ablaze in color. On the lower slopes, mountain laurel blooms in May; higher up, from mid-June to July. Flame azaleas bloom in late-June on Andrews Bald, the highest bald in the Smokies; hybrid azaleas on Gregory Bald in late June to early July; and purple (actually pinkish) and white rhododendrons are everywhere from mid-June through July.

Secret Information

For more facts about the balds of the Smokies, read "The Treeless Places" in Rose Houk's *Great Smoky Mountains National Park: A Natural History Guide* (Houghton Mifflin, 1993). The book offers a thorough look at the park's flora and fauna as well.

TOP SECRET

The easiest hike to one of the mysterious grassy balds in the Great Smoky Mountains National Park is the one to Andrews Bald, a round-trip of just over three and a half miles. Park in the Clingmans Dome parking lot. Follow the blacktop trail, then turn onto the Forney Ridge trail. The first half mile is a moderately steep and rocky downhill slope, but the rest of the trail is an easy walk. You'll be starting out at 6,250 feet elevation, descend to about 5,700 feet, then climb again to about 5,900 at the bald itself, which in late spring is covered with blooming flame azaleas and Catawba rhododendrons.

42

Seafood Roundup

Dot Goins describes her late husband, Murrel, as an avid fisherman and a flashy dresser. He and Dot owned a cabin near Douglas Lake, in Tennessee, just north of the Great Smoky Mountains National Park; and over the years the fellows he fished with there started calling him "Cowboy" because of the Stetson-style hat he always wore.

Cowboy also liked to cook. In the early seventies, he opened a tiny twenty-five-seat eatery on the lake to cater to his fishing buddies. Soon, however, folks were lining up to feast on huge platters of fried and broiled fish. Even after the original building burned down in 1979, local anglers remembered Cowboys so fondly that they begged Cowboy to reopen it, which he finally did in 1986. He ran it until 1994, when he passed away. Today the spot is still the place to eat seafood on the lake, although Dot has renamed it Cowboys on the Water because "It sounds classier."

What we like about Cowboys on the Water is that it's a true fish house like those found in New England or on the Carolina coast. There are the requisite stuffed bass and barracuda, fishing poles, and ship steering wheels hanging on the walls, although mixed with western memorabilia and pictures of the dearly departed founder. When Cowboy expanded the original restaurant, he opened the place before the floor was finished: He just threw down some cedar shavings instead. Not much has changed since then. The floor is still covered with sawdust and guests snack on peanuts and toss the shells wherever they want. Drinks are served in Mason jars. Dress is casual, although a warning to sun-bathing boaters reads, "Shirts and shoes required." The clientele are primarily repeat customers. "We don't advertise a lot," Dot says. "People find us mostly by word of mouth."

The most popular item on the menu is the formidable fried or broiled seafood platter, which features practically the entire cast of

Cowboys on the Water is a true fish house and it actually does face a lake.

The Little Mermaid—eight shrimp, one deviled crab, a quarter pound of clam strips, and two flounder filets (the platter for two simply doubles that). On the slightly lighter side are selections like catfish filets, grilled orange roughy smothered in butter, and Alaskan snow crab legs. Several surf and turf combos also are available.

Besides an ocean of seafood options, the restaurant's other big attraction is the view of Douglas Lake. The white-frame building is right on the water, and its windows face not only the water but also a twelve-hundred-acre Tennessee Valley Authority-owned island. Boaters often cruise up to Cowboys' dock, tie up their vessels, and walk up the slight hill to have dinner.

Secret Information

Location: On Tennessee Highway 139, west of Dandridge, Tennessee.

Address: 1435 Highway 139, Dandridge, Tennessee 37725.

Phone: (423) 397-2529.

Hours: Summer: 4:30 P.M. to 9:30 P.M., Monday through Thursday; 4:00 P.M. to 10:00 P.M., Friday and Saturday; and 12:00 P.M. to 8:00 P.M., Sunday. Winter: 4:30 P.M. to 8:30 P.M., Monday through Thursday; 4:00 P.M. to 9:00 P.M., Friday and Saturday; and 12:00 P.M. to 8:00 P.M., Sunday.

Reservations: Not accepted.

Prices: Entrees range from $7.97 to $22.95; sandwiches from $4.50 to $6.95; kids menu $2.50 to $4.50.

Credit cards: American Express, Discover, MasterCard, Visa.

Details: No alcohol served.

TOP SECRET

The owner of Cowboys on the Water, Dot Goins, lives next door to the restaurant and operates a tiny "nice and quiet" six-unit motel that caters to fishermen. "People who stay in our motel don't want to leave," she says. Call the restaurant for rates and reservations.

Home Sweet Home **43**

When Ralph and Dot Egli first opened Mountain Laurel Chalets in 1972, there were only a handful of chalet-rental outfits in Gatlinburg, Tennessee. Most of the mountainside homes were hidden in the trees well off of Wiley Oakley and Ski Mountain Roads. They were the lodgings of choice for honeymooners seeking a secluded hideaway: With only trees for neighbors, it was easy to sunbathe or soak in the buff in the outside hot tub. When you rented a chalet, you really were renting privacy and peace.

Mountain Laurel has been joined by dozens of other chalet-rental companies. If you ride the tram up to Ober Gatlinburg, instead of trees you'll see a mountainside of green, red, and black roofs. The chalet building boom of the last twenty-five years has claimed most buildable slopeside lots on Ski Mountain, plus a few that don't seem too safe to build on. The Eglis have witnessed all the construction and even added some of the new chalets to their rental list. Over the past twenty-five years they've moved to a bigger office and reprinted their timeless manila-colored illustrated (no glossy color pictures) brochure several times. Beyond that, not much has changed in the way they did business back before the boom and the way they do it now. Their Mountain Laurel Chalets was one of the first, and when it comes to choosing a place to rent a chalet above Gatlinburg, first is best.

The newer chalets, built one after another on the roadside in plain view of passing cars, or precariously perched on bald ridges where all the trees have been cleared, simply can't compete in terms of setting and seclusion with Mountain Laurel favorites like the A-frame Pine Top, with its forest-view Jacuzzi, and the circular Fantasia, with its panoramic vistas of the mountains. Although the majority of Mountain Laurel's chalets are a decade or older, all are up-to-date and include a full kitchen with dishwasher, central heat and air, cable TV, either a gas or wood-burning fireplace, and free swimming and

The Gatlinburg area is legendary for its mountainside homes, cabins, and chalets, and Mountain Laurel Chalets offers an ideal spot for honeymooners and other romantics. (Photo courtesy of Mountain Laurel Chalets)

tennis at mountainside clubhouses. Several chalets are equipped with whirlpools or hot tubs, VCRs, game tables, and washer/dryers.

Once you check in at Mountain Laurel on Ski Mountain Road, there's really no reason to battle the stop-and-go Gatlinburg traffic for the rest of your vacation. The chalets are all situated on Ski Mountain, and it's a straight shot down Ski Mountain Road to the Great Smoky Mountains National Park entrance at Sugarlands. If you want to sneak back into Pigeon Forge one night for some go-cart racing or miniature golf, take the Gatlinburg Bypass (Secret 10) off the mountain and avoid the town's traffic altogether. Once you arrive in Pigeon Forge and see that long concrete row of motel after motel, you might just turn around and hightail it back up the mountain. That's one of the hazards of getting away from it all in a Mountain Laurel chalet—once you've experienced true peace and quiet, it's tough to go back to the real world.

Secret Information

Location: On Ski Mountain Road (traffic light number 10), in Gatlinburg, Tennessee.

Address: 440 Ski Mountain Road, Gatlinburg, Tennessee 37738.

Phone: (800) 626-3431 or (423) 436-6434.

E-mail: info@mtnlaurelchalets.com.

Web site: www.mtnlaurelchalets.com.

Season: Year-round.

Rates: $90 to $585 a night.

Credit cards: American Express.

Details: Mountain Laurel Chalets rents one hundred properties ranging in size from one to eleven bedrooms. A two-night minimum is required, except for July and October, when it's three nights, and Thanksgiving when it's four.

TOP SECRET

There are no rental chalets in the Great Smoky Mountains National Park, but Mountain Laurel Chalets has the next best thing—Southern Exposure. This three-bedroom, two-bath chalet sits right next to the park border and offers completely unobstructed views of the park. Listen to the birds and watch for bear and deer while sitting in the outdoor hot tub, or challenge your companions to a friendly game of foosball. The traditional Bavarian-look chalet also includes two TVs, a VCR, a CD player, and a carport, plus all the regular chalet amenities. It costs $140 per night for two people and is situated near the end of Zurich Road on Ski Mountain.

One-Stop Adventure

Some people come to the Smokies to sit back and savor the wilderness. Others like to attack it head-on. The latter come here looking for hard-charging adventure that challenges nature and themselves. For the folks whose idea of a perfect vacation is a heart-pumping run down a raging river, a muscle-burning bike ride through the mountains, or another action-packed activity, there's no better place to go than to the Nantahala Outdoor Center.

NOC, as everyone calls it, is king of area outfitters, offering a one-stop spot for adventure vacations. It's headquartered in a complex situated at the convergence of the Appalachian Trail and Nantahala River just southwest of Bryson City, North Carolina. An employee-owned operation, it opened in 1972 in an old gas station and greasy spoon restaurant on the site now occupied by its operations buildings, 132-bed lodge, three restaurants, outfitter's store, and day-care center.

NOC is headed by sixty-three-year-old Payson Kennedy, CEO and resident "philosopher," a former computer specialist who was among the company's founders. His philosophical outlook concerns a "flow state" in which there is complete focus on, and absolute absorption in, an activity. All that means is that he and his staff of one hundred year-round employees and four hundred or so in-season staff members are driven by a passion for outdoor adventure, not pure profit. Employees are uniformly enthusiastic and love what they're doing. The president of NOC, for example, is Bunny Johns, a past champion white-water canoe racer who has spent thirty years in paddle sports and twenty-two years as a guide and instructor at the outfitter. Although she manages the $15-million-plus enterprise that NOC has become, she still takes paddlers out a couple of days a week. Staff and customers form such close bonds as they experience adventures together that each October the NOC throws its Guest Appreciation Festival, a kind of Woodstock of wilderness adventure.

A Nantahala raft trip can be a real rush. (Arvilla Brewer photo courtesy of Nantahala Outdoor Center)

Mountain biking at Nantahala can give whole new meaning to "going for the burn." (Arvilla Brewer photo courtesy of Nantahala Outdoor Center)

NOC adventures, however, aren't just for athletic and experienced outdoorspeople. It offers programs for every age and experience level. The five southeastern rivers used for white-water rafting—Nantahala, French Broad, Nolichucky, Ocoee, and Chattooga—range from relatively mild water, right for families, to raging rapids. Its world-renowned paddling school gives instruction to those who've never even sat down in a canoe or kayak. Mountain biking opportunities on more than forty miles of single-track trails include a camp just for kids. The center also offers teamwork-building adventure courses—including rope work and rappelling—for corporate and youth groups. To misquote the navy's slogan: At NOC, it's not just a vacation, it's an adventure.

Secret Information

Location: On U.S. Highway 19/74, southwest of Bryson City, North Carolina.
Address: 13077 Highway 19 West, Bryson City, North Carolina 28713-9114.
Phone: (704) 488-2175 or (888) 662-1662.
Fax: (704) 488-2498.
E-mail: rafting@noc.com (for rafting information).
Web site: www.nocweb.com.
Season: March through mid-November.
Prices: Rafting trips range from $15 to $198 per person. Check with NOC for prices of other activities.
Reservations: Required.
Credit cards: Discover, MasterCard, Visa.

TOP SECRET

Yearning to go sea kayaking off the coasts of Ireland or Greece? Want to go white-water rafting in Chile or Nepal? The Nantahala Outdoor Center's world of adventure stretches far beyond the Great Smoky Mountains to include adventure treks to exotic locations around the globe. Prices for trips within America and abroad start at about $800. For more information, call (704) 488-2175, ext. 333, or send e-mail to adtrav@noc.com.

Hedgewood Gardens

Wildflower Wonders

45

To show what an intrepid naturalist her mother was, Hope Woodard likes to tell what she calls "the snake story." Despite her family's repeated pleas not to go off into the wilderness alone, her elderly mom, Hedy Woodard, was forever disappearing into the Smokies in search of exotic flora and fauna.

"One day she'd driven into a remote cove, when a couple of gruff-looking men pulled up beside her car, got out, and approached her," Woodard says. "Mom was a bit fearful, and when they asked what she was doing, she replied, 'Glad you asked!' and showed them a gunny sack she held. She then announced that inside the sack was a rattlesnake that she had captured and that she was collecting venom for the University of Tennessee. At that point the gunny sack appeared to wiggle. She offered to show the men just how she captured the snakes and how she collected the venom, but they quickly excused themselves and left."

When Hedy Woodard wasn't collecting reptiles, she was in the woods gathering native plants for transplanting to the area around her home in Townsend, Tennessee. An artist and expert on the medicinal uses of Mother Nature's offspring, she spent twenty-two years creating a garden covering six acres and featuring the densest concentration of different blooming plants found anywhere in the Smokies—more than five hundred species in all. Today the site is called Hedgewood Gardens, so named for Hedy and her husband, George Wood. The grand gardener's commitment to nurturing nature and educating others about it is being carried on by her daughter.

Hope guides groups of schoolchildren, church members, or tourists on nature walks along winding trails through a colorful kaleidoscope of bloodroot, Saint-John's-wort, bee balm, yellow lady's slipper, great white trillium, wood anemone, hepatica, butterfly weed, bellworts, mountain laurel, rhododendron, wild geranium, blue and yellow flag iris, crested wood iris, and more. She'll stop along the way and tell the story behind a particular piece of greenery like jack-in-the-pulpit, a plant that changes sex if the soil conditions aren't right for the female to reproduce. April and May, of course, are the best time to catch flowers in their full glory, but something is in bloom almost all year round.

Woodard runs Hedgewood Gardens with an emphasis on education for people living in the area and those with a real desire to learn and with an appreciation of natural settings. She wants the gardens to grow slowly to keep everything natural. It is purposely not highly advertised, and tours are available by appointment only. Her plans for future expansion include placing easels with her mother's paintings around the garden, blending art and nature, and reopening Hedy's art gallery, which is now used only for storage. She'd also like to create a large pond and build an open pavilion for picnics and expand the classes she has already started.

Secret Information

Location: On Bethel Church Road, off U.S. Highway 321, in Townsend, Tennessee.
Address: 411 Bethel Church Road, Townsend, Tennessee 37882.
Phone: (423) 984-2052 (Hope Woodard's home).
Hours: Tours are by appointment only; call Hope Woodard at her home.
Prices: $2–$4 per person.
Credit cards: None.

TOP SECRET

Dale Rice lives on the Hedgewood Gardens property and tends the grounds. He also keeps a collection of raptors—birds of prey—that have been injured and cannot be released into the wild. He frequently presents educational programs about them around the Smoky Mountains area. Ask Hope Woodard to try to arrange for you to see these beautiful and intimidating birds as part of a tour.

Parson Branch Road

Open Road

46

The deluge came in Spring 1994, when, in just thirty-six hours, parts of the Smokies received nine inches of rain. Creeks and streams throughout the Great Smoky Mountains National Park overflowed their banks and washed out several roads, most prominently the Little River Road that connects Gatlinburg and Townsend, Tennessee. That route and others were repaired within the following few years, with the last one, Parson Branch Road, scheduled for reopening in 1998.

This dirt and gravel route from Cades Cove to U.S. Highway 129 on the southwest side of the park almost remained permanently closed. Environmental groups opposed to routes through the wilderness pressured the park service to leave it as Mother Nature's downpour intended, but locals rallied support to rebuild the eight-mile-long historic wagon route to North Carolina that was first established in the 1830s and is one of only two original ways out of the cove.

Like Heintooga-Round Bottom Road (Secret 88), Parson Branch is accessible for those who like to drive, rather than hike, into the heart of a primeval forest. While the road is narrow, one-way, low-standard, and low-speed, it's likely to be comfortable for those in two-wheel-drive cars and passenger vans, because of the recent repairs. Running almost in the streambed of Parson Branch Creek, the road starts near the Cades Cove Visitor Center and is sometimes winding and steep. The high point on the drive is at 2,780 feet at Sam's Gap on Hannah Mountain, a popular spot where people can park and make the four-mile hike to Gregory Bald. From there the road travels down the mountains through a shady gorge of relatively undisturbed forest, pristine trout streams, and dense rhododendron, occasionally crossing low-water fords. Wildlife sightings include wild turkeys and black bears. At U.S. Highway 129, travelers have the option of heading west toward the Foothills Parkway (Secret 68) or east toward Fontana Village (Secret 12).

Even before the rain, Parson Branch was barely discovered, drawing only four to ten thousand vehicles a year. "It really is a secret" says Great Smoky Mountains National Park spokesperson Bob Miller. "Every year millions of people come into Cades Cove, and 99 percent of them go out the same way they came in." With the re-opening of Parson Branch Road, however, those with a more adventurous spirit and a strong suspension will have another way to get out of the traffic to sample a more remote slice of the Smokies.

Secret Information

Location: Off Forge Creek Road, which starts at the Cades Cove Visitor Center at Cable Mill, about midway around the Cades Cove loop.

Details: Parson Branch Road was scheduled to reopen to automobile traffic in mid-1998. Call the Great Smoky Mountains National Park at (423) 436-1200 for an exact date. The road is closed during the winter.

TOP SECRET

Among those who fought to have Parson Branch Road reopened are mountain bikers. Bicycling is allowed only on developed roads in the Great Smoky Mountains National Park, and there are few options for those who love to challenge themselves by climbing rugged hills or gripping the handlebars for dear life while hurtling down steep slopes. The repaired Parson Branch should be perfect for hard-core cyclists, but check with the park service first to make sure it's open to cyclers.

The Museum of Appalachia

History on Display

47

The Museum of Appalachia isn't in the Smokies, but nowhere from Cosby to Cades Cove or from Cherokee to Cataloochee can you get a better feel for the mountains and their people.

The museum is in the Tennessee Valley Authority-created town of Norris, Tennessee, about twenty-five miles north of Knoxville on Interstate 75. Actually, the tag *museum* doesn't really do this place justice. It's nothing like a musty mausoleum filled with art, but a living open-air labor of love-in-progress by local author and historian John Rice Irwin. Sixty-five lush acres of farmland (complete with grazing goats, sheep, horses, peacocks, hens, and turkeys) surround thirty-plus structures housing more than two hundred fifty thousand Appalachian artifacts. Irwin has heard a million mountain stories, and, luckily for all of us, he has captured them in words and objects for all to see.

One of the newest additions is the 'Possum Trot, Tennessee, cabin, where more than likely Mark Twain was conceived. He was born five months after his family moved to its new home in Missouri. Another one-room, dirt-floored, log building dating back to the early 1800s is known as the Dan'l Boone Cabin because it was used by 20th Century Fox in the CBS-TV series *Young Dan'l Boone*.

You can spend a few hours strolling the grounds and sittin' for a spell on the rockin' chair porch of the Peters Homestead to hear local mountain musicians make magic on the fiddle and guitar. Or you can spend all day in the Museum of Appalachia Hall of Fame Building, if you read every little hand-printed display card. From the outside, this elegant three-story brick building looks like any historic home in Gettysburg or Williamsburg, but the inside is like stepping into some highly motivated kid's school project. The place is packed to the rafters with relics belonging to the region's famous and not-so-famous folks, plus Indian artifacts, hundreds of early musical instruments, tools, and just plain off-the-wall items—all

The Museum of Appalachia isn't one of your typical musty mausoleum-types; it's an open-air layout with more than thirty structures housing more than 250,000 Appalachian artifacts.

with personal stories of where they came from and how Mr. Irwin acquired them.

"What better way is there to know a people than to study the everyday things they made, used, mended, and cherished . . . and cared for with loving hands.—JRI," reads the hand-painted message from Irwin above the Hall of Fame's first display area. Below is an eclectic mix of artifacts, including Uncle Jim McCoy's handmade bear trap and Uncle Henry Moss's peg leg. Across the way are exhibits honoring Grandpa Jones, the Carter Family, and a fiddler named Bob Douglas, who was nine years old when he got his first pair of shoes, seventy-five when he won first place at the National Folklife Fiddle Contest, and over ninety when he brought his cherished boyhood fiddle to the museum.

To explore at a leisurely pace without a lot of other folks around, visit midweek, either early in the morning or late in the afternoon. If you don't mind mobs of people, check out the Tennessee Fall Homecoming (the second full weekend in October) for a true taste of mountain music, crafts, and culture. There are shepherding demonstrations,

One of the museum's recent additions is the cabin in which it is believed Mark Twain was conceived.

fiddlin', storytelling, every kind of Appalachian craft, and our favorite, anvil shoots (take one anvil, place atop explosives, light the fuse, and see how far it flies into the air). As our kids would say, "Cool!"

Secret Information

> *Location:* East of I-75 (exit 122), on Tennessee Highway 61 in Norris, Tennessee.
> *Address:* Highway 61, Norris, Tennessee 37828.
> *Phone:* (423) 494-7680.
> *Hours:* 8:00 A.M. until dark, daily, except Christmas.
> *Prices:* $6 for adults; $4 for children, ages 6 to 15; free for children under 6; seniors $5.

Credit cards: MasterCard, Visa.

TOP SECRET

Visit the museum late in the day on Thursday, then cross the street to Patsy's Cafe and Music Center for supper and free bluegrass music by local musicians (including some who play at the museum). Patsy's is a small brown barnboard house with a wide front porch that accommodates pickers and patrons alike. There's a hand-painted orange-lettered sign on the roof that reads "Patsy's Home Cookin'."

48

Standing the Test of Time

Nothing much has changed at the Fryemont Inn since 1923. Thank goodness. In these parts, folks tend to take an "if it ain't broke, don't fix it" approach to life. There's nothing modern or fancy or state-of-the-art about the Fryemont.

When timber baron Amos Frye commissioned New York architect Richard Hunt (the same fellow who designed another North Carolina house called Biltmore) to build an "inn of rustic elegance," only the best local chestnut, oak, and maple trees were used for the structure and the furnishings. The exterior was protected with sturdy bark strips from massive old-growth poplar trees. Stone masons lugged rocks up from the Tuskasegee River to craft huge fireplaces in the lobby and dining room.

A single step into the spacious 1,850-square-foot lobby and family room takes you back seventy years. The fire in the massive hearth (it can hold eight-foot-long logs, though the flames are gas powered now) dances off the gleaming hardwood floors. Guests gather on antique couches and chairs to play checkers and cards and to hold heated battles with wooden skittles. French doors lead onto a broad rocking-chair porch, where guests sip complimentary tea and coffee and look down on the twinkling lights of Bryson City, North Carolina, below.

Strolling down one warm, wood-paneled guest-room corridor leads visitors to a well-worn footpath that winds to the secluded swimming pool nestled in the dogwoods and hemlocks. A walk down the other corridor ends in the dining room with its raftered vaulted ceiling and brass-and-wood paddle fans. Back in the twenties and thirties, the Fryemont was the place in Bryson City for dances, and the dining room was where groups like the Original Hotel Gordon Orchestra would perform every Thursday. Admission was $1.50 for men; ladies got in free. Today's Fryemont Inn guests dine on scrumptious country and mountain fare, including fresh mountain trout fixed at least four different ways and Vidalia onion casserole for dinner. Breakfast features stacks of flapjacks and warm baskets of blueberry muffins—all included in the room rate.

When Amos Frye first welcomed guests back in 1923, he catered to a rich clientele. City folks from up and down the East Coast flocked to his inn to be pampered. Nowadays, the Fryemont Inn welcomes anyone searching for a place to make time stop for a day or two. Backpackers, hikers, kayakers, and those most fearless of adventurers—parents with young children—all fit nicely. Leave behind your suits, ties, skirts, and heels.

Secret Information

Location: Bryson City, North Carolina.

Address: 1 Fryemont Road, Bryson City, North Carolina 28713; mailing address: P.O. Box 459, Bryson City, North Carolina 28713.

Phone: (704) 488-2159.

Rates: (depending on season): Queen-size bed for one $70 to $82; queen-size bed for two $92 to $108; king-size bed for two $102 to $120; two double beds for two to four $102 to $120; family suite with two bedrooms for three $146 to $172 plus $30 per adult or $18 per child up to a total of six people.

Credit cards: Discover, MasterCard, Visa.

Season: The inn is open mid-April to November 1; adjacent modern cottage suites are open year-round.

Details: There are no televisions or telephones in the guest rooms and no air conditioning.

TOP SECRET

Each of the thirty-seven chestnut-paneled guest rooms at the Fryemont Inn is charming, but the single queen-bed quarters can get a little cramped for two hearty-eating adults. Room 230 upstairs on the front side of the inn is a long room that offers views of the pines, the mountains, and Bryson City; and it has two double beds, desk, and a sitting area that provides ample room for reading and relaxing.

49

Down on the Farm

Brookhaven Farm rests gently on two hundred lush and wooded acres in the foothills of the Smokies, halfway between Knoxville and Gatlinburg, Tennessee. Back in the fifties, when the Brooks family built their spread and started curing country hams, they regularly invited neighbors over for a morning ham biscuit. After word about the Brookses' tasty brand of country ham soon spread around the surrounding community of Seymour and on to south Knoxville, the family opened a small farmhouse restaurant on their property. When some folks from Knoxville balked at the idea of driving all the way out to the backwoods of Seymour for a meal, the Brookses leased a bus to pick up and deliver the customers to the farmhouse's front porch.

The Brooks family no longer own the property, but their name and tradition of inviting everyone over to enjoy their land and bounty remain. The farm's picnic, reception, and lodging facilities are available all week for corporate parties, weddings, family reunions, and such, but Sunday from 11:00 A.M. until 3:00 P.M. is when regular folks once again get to enjoy the open space and restful pace of the farm at the all-you-can-eat country breakfast buffet.

Couples sit on the sheltered porch swings reading their Sunday *Knoxville News-Sentinel*s and *Atlanta Journal-Constitution*s while their children play *Little House on the Prairie* in the log cabin playhouse, complete with loft and swing. Inside the country-accented function hall (the original farmhouse restaurant was destroyed by fire in 1992), guests chow down on southern favorites like homemade biscuits and gravy, meat loaf, fried chicken, hash browns with bits of bacon, scrambled eggs, and mashed potatoes. There's a bountiful salad, vegetable, and fruit bar, and a central table piled high with freshly baked desserts such as strawberry shortcake and fruit cobbler.

Most folks who come out Sunday are part of the greater

Knoxville area's after-church crowd. They're looking for a place to enjoy a leisurely meal while gazing out the big picture windows at a perfect pastoral scene—rolling lawns surrounding a small sparkling lake in which flocks of Canada geese congregate.

Unlike chain restaurants, Brookhaven Farm isn't out to haul in a huge profit from its buffet. In fact, the farm now is a not-for-profit operation run by Knoxville's Child and Family Services, a United Way-funded social service organization. "Any profits the farm earns go to help children through a wide range of services from counseling to runaway shelters," says Freddy Kistner, the assistant general manager at Brookhaven.

Secret Information

Location: Off Burnett Station Road, south of Seymour, Tennessee.
Address: 604 Brookhaven Lane, Seymour, Tennessee 37865.
Phone: (423) 579-7979.
Hours: Country buffet 11:00 A.M. until 3:00 P.M., Sunday.
Prices: Adults $7.95; children $3.95; under 4 years free.
Credit cards: Visa.

TOP SECRET

An added, yet unadvertised, bonus for buffet guests at Brookhaven Farm is the complimentary use of its fishing and paddleboating pond, Lake Erin. After Sunday brunch, stroll down the gravel path past the geese to the boathouse. There are life jackets, paddleboats, canoes, and cane poles with hooks and bobbers all there for your use—free of charge. All fishing is done on a catch-and-release basis, so your kids can experience the excitement of having a smallmouth bass or carp tugging on their line without seeing the poor guy get filleted and fried. Other days of the week visitors can drop by to use the boats, canoes, and fishing poles for about $5 per person. Call (423) 579-7979 for details.

50 Family Floating

Ask anyone, "Where's the best spot to go tubing on the Tennessee side of the Smokies?" and more often than not the answer will be "the Y near Townsend." Just inside the Great Smoky Mountains National Park, it's a spot where the road splits one way toward Gatlinburg and the other toward Cades Cove. It's also where two prongs of the Little River merge into a big pool, then pass out of the park to flow through the tiny town of Townsend and beyond. The converging water makes it a prime spot to stick your behind through an inner tube and plunge into the chilly creek. Float aimlessly down the river paddling furiously only when nearing a big clump of rocks or a menacing-looking baby waterfall.

Unfortunately, the Y draws hordes of people. On sweltering summer days the banks of the river are filled with blankets, coolers, lawn chairs, radios, and other man-made touches that interfere with a relaxing day on the water. And then there are the bodies—many of the big beer-belly variety—plunging off the nearby rock ledges perilously close to the tubers.

We prefer to stay away from the Y and tube a bit farther downstream in Townsend proper. Right at the point where U.S. Highway 321 (Secret 55) cuts east toward Wears Valley is River Romp Tubes, which is part of a shop called Body Wear Outlet. While there are several mom-and-pop places to rent plain black inner tubes for a little less money elsewhere on the way to the national park, we like River Romp because they rent only safety-approved water-ski tubes. The pink and purple colors are cool to kids and cool to the touch compared with the traditional black rubber tubes. Also, if you have a child under the age of six, you can request a tube with a cord attached so you can float safely in tandem. Unlike some other tube-renting spots, River Romp issues every child a life jacket, custom-fitted at the store. It's nice that you can choose to pay extra for the float-and-tote

Plenty of tubes are available for rental at Body Wear Outlet.

option, which means the River Romp shuttle will pick you up at the put-out point and bring you back upstream for another run.

Just behind the shop is a great place to put into the water well downstream from the cannonballers and other distractions of the Y. The section of river you'll tube is clear of debris, partying yahoos, and bunches of bodies. Sure, the tree-lined shore isn't wilderness, as it is within the park, but it's a lot more peaceful. It's home to ducks, blue herons, and wildflowers. Float along behind small vacation cabins and wave at locals picnicking on their porches suspended above the river. The rapids give you a good bumpy ride in a couple of spots, but you and your family can for the most part sit back and soak up the sun without fear of unheavenly bodies dropping out of the sky on you.

Secret Information

Location: River Romp is at the intersection where U.S. Highway 321/Tennessee Highway 73 heads northeast into Wears Valley from Townsend, Tennessee.

Address: 8203 State Highway 73, Townsend, Tennessee 37822.

Phone: (423) 448-1522.

Hours: 10:00 A.M. to 6:00 P.M., Sunday through Friday; 9:00 A.M. to 6:00 P.M., Saturday.

Season: Memorial Day through Labor Day.

Prices: $5 per tube; $10 per tube for pickup and ride back to the store.

Credit cards: Discover, MasterCard, Visa.

TOP SECRET

Townsend is the most popular tubing spot on the Tennessee side of the Smokies, but it's not the only one. To get away from the national park and the hordes of people it draws, rent tubes at Little Pigeon Tubing, which is just off Pittman Center Road on the back way to and from Gatlinburg (Secret 10). Prices are higher than in Townsend—$11 for adults, $7 for children—but they include ski tubes (ones with bottoms available for children), life vests, and a ride from the end of the two-mile tubing run on the Little Pigeon River back to your car. During the late spring and summer, call (423) 428-TUBE (8823) or (800) 690-0972 for more information and to be sure they are open (phones are disconnected the rest of the year). They close if there has been too little rain to keep the river running rapidly.

Lulu's Cafe

A Lulu of a Meal

51

When Louise Turner opened up her storefront cafe in sleepy downtown Sylva, North Carolina, locals were less than impressed. Maybe it was the rose-colored walls or the crimson ceiling fans that scared them. Or maybe it was the art deco green and purple neon sign in the window. Or more likely it was the wildly creative menu featuring only fresh ingredients in dishes with names such as Artichoke-Montrachet Crostine or Indonesian Shrimp Satay.

"If your food wasn't fried, barbecued, or made with fat back then, people around here thought you had to be weirdoes," says the slim blonde hostess who quite obviously "ain't from around here" and would rather remain nameless so she can keep her day job. "It's taken awhile for us to become accepted. I'm sure some of them still think we're weird, but they have to admit the food is the best."

Lulu's menu bills its offerings as "food that looks as good as it tastes," and it looks superb. The Caribbean black beans served on a bed of saffron rice with grilled plantains is a confetti-colored concoction meant to be savored by both the eyes and the palate. Although the most creative menu items appeal mainly to adults, Lulu's Cafe is top-shelf in quality and inventiveness only—not in attitude or price. Children are welcome and any family that has subsisted on fast food during their vacation owes their digestive system a lunch or dinner at Lulu's Cafe. Not only are the children's meals inexpensive ($2.50 and under), none are served with fries. A mom-pleasing mini fresh-fruit salad accompanies the burger, provolone pita melt, and the marinated chicken.

The lone dining room at Lulu's is intimate, with chic black baseboards, black booths, and black-and-white wall photos highlighted by iced sconce lights. The green chairs and door and floral tablecloths give the interior the feel of a shady English country garden. The feel of a chic bistro has made Lulu's a favorite spot for stars who are making movies in western North Carolina to hang out. Kevin Bacon was actually filming *Digging to China* clear over on the other corner of the Smokies at Fontana, when he and his wife found their way across winding mountain roads to Lulu's on several occasions. And while making *The Fugitive* nearby, Harrison Ford became such a fixture at Lulu's that he finally had to retreat from the adoring fans at the cafe and ask the chef to prepare meals for him at his rental home.

Secret Information

Location: Downtown Sylva, North Carolina.
Address: 612 West Main Street, Sylva, North Carolina 28779.
Phone: (704) 586-8989.
Hours: 11:00 A.M. until 9:00 P.M., during the summer; 11:00 A.M. to 8:00 P.M., Monday through Thursday, and 11:00 A.M. to 9:00 P.M. Friday and Saturday, during the winter.
Prices: Dinner entrees from $8.95 to $15.95; lunch entrees $2.25 to $7.25.
Credit cards: MasterCard, Visa.
Details: Named "our favorite restaurant in the region" by *Southern Living* magazine.

TOP SECRET

After a meal at Lulu's Cafe, walk up the hill to the City Lights Bookstore and Cafe at 3 East Jackson Street in Sylva. Inside the softly lit wood and white-walled interior of the funky white trilevel house enveloped by wildflowers are found folk music, fabulous desserts and coffees, and a haphazard collection of small rooms lined with new and used books. From 8:00 P.M. until 10:00 P.M. every Friday and Saturday night, plus the occasional Thursday, there's free entertainment in the downstairs cafe. If you're lucky, you can snag a table in the outdoor courtyard and enjoy the mochaccino and the music alfresco.

For a rookie hiker, the thought of striking out alone on a Great Smoky Mountains National Park trail can seem a bit like slipping behind the wheel of a car for the first time. You're excited. You know that there's a big, wide wonderful world out there to explore; but you sure wish there was someone there beside you to point out the pitfalls, guide you down the road, and simply keep you company along the way.

Say hello to the Smoky Mountains Hiking Club. The six-hundred-plus-member organization has actually been around longer than the park itself. It was founded by eight East Tennessee men who embarked on the organization's first official hike—a Sunday afternoon stroll up 6,593-foot Mount LeConte in December 1924. They had been taking regular Sunday mountain treks sponsored by the Knoxville YMCA, but when the local Baptist establishment raised a ruckus about a Christian-affiliated group hiking and not hallelujahing on Sundays, the outdoorsmen decided to form their own nonaffiliated hiking club.

With the opening of the park in 1934, part of the Smoky Mountains Hiking Club's mission was complete, but the members never stopped trekking and teaching. Today the thriving club sponsors a full schedule of weekend and Wednesday hikes year-round, ranging from easy five-mile-and-under flatlander walks to challenging backcountry overnights. And here's the secret: All hikes are open to nonmembers.

"We're totally open to having visitors on every trip: Unfortunately, it would be pretty impossible for a visitor to show up at the Sugarlands Visitor Center in Gatlinburg and connect with one of our hikes," says Bill Kerr, a former club president and the current chairman of its Appalachian Trail committee.

Kerr encourages those who are planning trips to the Smokies to write to the hiking club in advance for its newsletter and/or handbook to find out what hikes are scheduled during their stay. The brief

Visitors to the Smokies are welcome to hike with the Smoky Mountains Hiking Club. (Photo courtesy of Great Smoky Mountains National Park)

hike descriptions provide an overview of the terrain covered, the scenery, the length of the hike, and the elevation gains. If you haven't arranged for a newsletter or a handbook in advance of your trip to the Smokies, call the club office in Knoxville, Tennessee. If you're interested in a particular upcoming trip, simply show up at the designated meeting place on the day and time listed and join the members; no reservation or fee is required. Be sure, however, to wear sturdy hiking boots and haul water and raingear in your backpack.

Visitors hiking with the Smoky Mountains Hiking Club can avoid the congestion and backpack-to-backpack hiking on some of the Smokies' most popular and easily accessible trails. Club hikes are both on- and off-trail and offer challenging climbs as well as cool, quiet walks along shady creeks. "I like walking along the creeks, but honestly, I've never been on a trail in the Smokies that wasn't a pleasant place to walk," Kerr says. "They're all special in their own way. There's really no expense in hiking and there's no question that it's the best—no, the only—way to see the Smokies."

Secret Information

Address: P.O. Box 1454, Knoxville, Tennessee 37901.

Phone: (423) 558-1341.

Prices: There is no charge to hike with the Smoky Mountains Hiking Club. The monthly newsletter is $10 per year and the club handbook, which lists the members' names and addresses and the hike schedule, is $4. Membership is open to anyone who participates in three club activities and pays the $14 annual fee, which also includes the newsletter and handbook. You do not have to live in the area to be either a member or a subscriber.

TOP SECRET

Help preserve the Smokies for future generations by spending one day of your vacation helping the Smoky Mountains Hiking Club tidy up the Appalachian Trail. The club, which actually helped blaze the section of the AT that passes through the Smokies, is responsible for maintaining the one hundred miles of trail in the Great Smoky Mountains National Park. The first Saturday of every month is an AT workday, and we do mean work: Club members and guests haul off brush and downed trees, pick up trash, move boulders, and do whatever it takes to keep the trail clean and clear. Contact the club for more information.

Reaching the Promised Land

It's only fitting that Mount Pisgah gets its name from the mountain mentioned in the Bible as the spot from which Moses first viewed the Promised Land. If you take the Blue Ridge Parkway all the way from its end point in the Great Smoky Mountains National Park back toward Asheville, North Carolina, and happen upon the Pisgah Inn, you'll feel like you've found heaven—or at least the perfect spot to stop, eat, explore, and stretch your legs after driving the scenic, yet long and winding, road.

The Pisgah Inn could even be a corn dog shack, and most Blue Ridge Parkway travelers would be happy for the chance to slurp a Coke and use the rest room. But this National Park Service concession is far more than a quick pit stop. Built in 1918 and opened in 1920 as the Original Pisgah Forest Inn, the simple gray wood, fifty-two-room inn and separate dining room, coffee shop, and gift shop was perched on Pisgah Ledge, 4,925 feet above sea level, for seventy-two years. Safety concerns then forced its demolition. The original main building was replaced with an equally simple rustic structure with three walls of windows, giving diners an unobstructed view of the mountains and balds below.

The view by itself (especially in the autumn) is worth the five bucks paid for a sandwich or even the eighteen dollars for the filet mignon, although the food is worth the trek. Many local folks come from Asheville or Waynesville just to dine at the Pisgah. You haven't eaten in the mountains until you sit under the wooden vaulted ceiling at the inn and have a fresh charbroiled mountain trout expertly filleted at your table or sample some locally cured country ham with a house special baked acorn squash in the shell.

After your meal, step into the Pisgah Inn's Craft Gallery featuring handmade crafts of the southern Appalachians. There are pottery, candles, jewelry, clothing, assorted gifts, and note cards with the lovable Pisgah Inn moose logo. The best buy, however, might be a hand-carved walking stick, because viewing the mountains from high atop the outdoor deck at the Pisgah Inn will definitely make you want to lace up your hiking boots and explore the beauty below—after some homemade caramel pie, of course.

Secret Information

Location: At mile marker 408 on the Blue Ridge Parkway in North Carolina.
Address: P.O. Box 749, Waynesville, North Carolina 28786.
Phone: (704) 235-8228.
Prices: Dinner entrees $6.50 to $17.95. Room rates $65 to $118.
Credit cards: MasterCard, Visa.

TOP SECRET

Hidden in the trees at the far end of the Pisgah Inn's parking lot is a trailhead with a map outlining the various hiking options. There are leisurely walks through the wilderness, challenging all-day hikes, as well as the 1.6-mile moderate-to-strenuous Mount Pisgah Trail, which leads to the summit and offers spectacular views of the French Broad River Valley and Shining Rock Wilderness. Before striking out on your hike, stop in at the Mount Pisgah Camp Store, adjacent to the parking lot, for a free handout describing each trail and to stock up on snacks. There are also rest rooms and a laundromat at the Camp Store.

54

Real Souvenirs
of the Smokies

The Smokies are filled with ticky-tacky souvenir shops that sell Appalachian-style arts and crafts, but if you want the real thing, head to the Arrowcraft Shop in the heart of Gatlinburg, Tennessee.

Housed in a shake-shingle building constructed in 1926 (by the way, it's the only shop in town with its own front lawn), the store is affiliated with the Arrowmont School of Arts and Crafts. Started in 1945 by the members of the Pi Beta Phi sorority, the school still teaches such skills as painting, drawing, textile making, metalworking, and woodworking to more than two thousand students a year. The Arrowcraft Shop, however, doesn't sell any pieces made by amateur artists. It stocks a wide range of traditional and contemporary items that are supplied by the Southern Highlands Craft Guild, a group of professional artists whose mission is the preservation and marketing of fine crafts. Headquartered in Asheville, North Carolina, the guild has seven hundred members and is the second-oldest crafts organization in the country. Members from nine states live mostly within one hundred miles of Arrowcraft, and the shop is a prime outlet for their work.

The atmosphere at Arrowcraft is peaceful. The sales staff seem more interested in explaining the history and tradition behind a piece than moving merchandise. The space is filled with baskets, hand puppets, leather goods, candles, stained glass, wrought iron, jewelry, birdhouses, brooms, handblown glass, pottery, ceramics, and every other kind of local work of art you could want. Small wonders are stashed everywhere. In a small room almost behind the cash register, for example, you'll find exquisite paper, which is created from beaten plant material, screened and pressed, then brushed to a smooth surface. The area showcases such creative artists as Claudia Lee of Kingsport, Tennessee, who takes handcrafted paper and molds it into clocks (her most popular item), wall decorations, pins, and stationery that's almost too beautiful to write on. All items sold at Arrowcraft are handmade (except for some small parts and fittings and a few books) and each is one of a kind. Prices range from a few dollars to thousands for museum-quality pieces like a finely woven white-oak basket or a hand-turned oak bowl. If you're shopping for a souvenir of your Smokies vacation, forget a Pigeon Forge T-shirt, fake raccoon hat, or *How to Speak Southern* and shoot straight to Arrowcraft Shop.

Secret Information

Location: Near stoplight number 6 on the Parkway in Gatlinburg, Tennessee.
Address: 576 Parkway, Gatlinburg, Tennessee 37738.
Phone: (423) 436-4604.
Hours: 9:00 A.M. to 9:00 P.M., Monday through Saturday; 9:00 A.M. to 6:00 P.M., Sunday.
Credit cards: Discover, MasterCard, Visa.

TOP SECRET

Right beside the Arrowcraft Shop is the home of its parent organization, the Arrowmont School of Arts and Crafts, an internationally known visual arts academy. For a fantastic learning vacation, take one of their one- or two-week spring or summer workshops in weaving, fabric design, pottery, photography, papermaking, or another artistic endeavor. Classes are about $260. No prior training is required, and you can even get college credit through the University of Tennessee. For more information, call the Arrowmont School at (423) 436-5860 or fax to (423) 430-4101.

55

The Long and Winding Road

Moving from place to place on the Tennessee side of the Smokies is as easy as 1-2-3, uh, we mean 321. U.S. Highway 321 winds and meanders east-west across the entire area. It travels through small cities and spectacular scenery, along nearly deserted rural roads and tourist-packed six-lane parkways, and through mountain passes and broad beautiful valleys. Take it to avoid much of the glut of vehicles that jam the more popular north-south routes.

The part of the route that runs through the Smokies stretches more than seventy-five miles from I-75 in the west to I-40 in the east. Rather than stick with the interstate to get to the heart of the Smokies, consider jumping off at exit 81 on I-75 or exit 364 on I-40 in Loudon County or exit 440 on I-40 in Newport and taking a more leisurely route to the mountains.

Heading from west to east, U.S. Highway 321 first passes through the small communities of Lenior City and Maryville (a cute little town whose main claim to fame is as the birthplace of presidential contender Lamar Alexander). Next it enters the foothills of the Smokies and heads toward Townsend, which accurately bills itself as "the peaceful side of the Smokies." Just as it appears about to enter the Great Smoky Mountains National Park, 321 takes a turn northeast into Wears Valley, a gorgeous gorge with just the right mix of open pastureland, rental cabins, and roadside shops.

On the other end of the valley, 321 combines with U.S. Highway 441 and heads south as part of the main, heavily trafficked drag into the Smokies. In contrast to the country quiet of Wears Valley, suddenly you're thrust into Pigeon Forge, a strip stuffed with every kind of tourist distraction you can imagine. Just south of Pigeon Forge, 321 heads into the mountains toward Gatlinburg, another tourist town that will never be as tacky as Pigeon Forge simply because it's a bit older and surrounded by so much natural beauty. Just as you enter town, 321 saves you from spending a few hours lurching between stoplights by once again shifting northeast and becoming far more rural as it takes you along the northern boundary of the national park. It travels through Cocke County (which is where the hard-core hillbillies live) and into the town of Newport, where you are reunited with the interstate system.

Secret Information

Secrets along the way include, among others: Carver's Orchard (Secret 57), Chef Jock's Tastebuds Cafe (Secret 92), Cosby Nature Trail (Secret 96), Earthtide School of Folk Arts (Secret 5), the Greenbrier Restaurant (Secret 77), Hedgewood Gardens (Secret 45), Hippensteal's Mountain View Inn (Secret 3), Holloway's Country Home (Secret 69), Mountain Laurel Chalets (Secret 43), Old Rose and Silver Tea Room (Secret 62), Ramsay Cascades (Secret 84), the Soda Fountain (Secret 36), the Front Porch Restaurant (Secret 1), Tuckaleechee Trout Farm Restaurant (Secret 67), and Von Bryan Inn (Secret 32).

TOP SECRET

On the Tennessee side, most folks head into the Great Smoky Mountains National Park through the main entrance at Gatlinburg. Others, a bit wiser, take the Townsend entrance. Few, however, know about the unmarked way in at Wears Valley. It's off U.S. Highway 321, about midway between Pigeon Forge and Townsend. Travel through the valley until you get to Line Springs Road and head south, even though there's no sign pointing the direction to the park entrance. In less than ten minutes, you'll be at Metcalf Bottoms Campground just off Little River Road. You will thus avoid the traffic backups getting into the park.

Locator Map

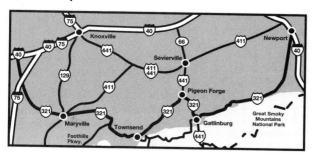

In the Shadow of the Smokies

Ginger Shinn was sixteen years old when her family stayed overnight at a mountaintop lodge in Maggie Valley, North Carolina, on a trip away from her home in Miami. Although she never got the chance to be a guest there again, Shinn often dreamed about the place with its roaring fireplace, deep winter snows, and winding hiking trails. When she married Bud Shinn several years later, she took him by the lodge a couple times, but they never stayed. Then one day fifteen years ago, the pair opened the *Miami Herald* to see a real estate ad for a mountaintop lodge in Maggie Valley.

"I told Bud, 'This has *got* to be Smokey Shadows,'" recalls Ginger, now a young grandmother. "It was like a dream. We bought the lodge and moved our family up here. It was like I was meant to come back here all along."

It's easy to see why Smokey Shadows (yes, that's Smokey with an *e*) made such a lasting impression on Shinn. The log and stone building is a former gristmill moved from its original Cataloochee Valley location to its picturesque perch, forty-five hundred feet above sea level. The view from the covered front porch, which runs the length of the lodge (Shinn thinks it should be billed as "the longest porch in the Smokies"), is arguably the most magnificent in Maggie Valley. Well-worn rockers, bird feeders, wind chimes, plants, and a sleeping cat give the porch a comfy feel conducive to midday napping. The sloping yard below is filled with flowers and leads to one of the many hiking trails that begin at the lodge.

The main lodge's twelve rooms are cozy and rustic. Log-beam ceilings and stone and log walls are accented by mountain quilt bedspreads and homemade curtains. The windows and doors are wormy chestnut, and the door handles are crafted from pieces of rawhide. No two rooms are alike. Several have feather beds, and many are decorated with antique hats that belonged to one of Bud's aunts. It's

Smokey Shadows Lodge was formerly a gristmill situated in Cataloochee Valley.

December all year in the Christmas Room with red, white, and green quilts on the twin beds and artificial pine wreaths on the walls. There are also two adjacent cabins, one more than a hundred years old, which can accommodate up to four guests each.

In the winter Shinn caters to youth groups who rent out the entire lodge and go skiing at nearby Cataloochee Ski Area (Secret 82). A fifteen-foot Christmas tree claims a corner of the vaulted-ceiling main room all of December, and the Shinns ferry guests who aren't comfortable tackling the sometimes snow- and ice-covered roads up the mountain. In spring and fall, the lodge hosts several wedding receptions and family reunions. The wood-ceiling country dining room, with its hardwood floors and antique stoves, copper pots, and baskets, is the site not only of parties but also of reservation-only dinners (roughly four nights a week) and a daily Continental breakfast for guests. "I love to entertain and cook, so the country weddings are really special for me," Shinn says as she discusses the night's dinner menu of angel hair pasta topped with herb-and-wine marinated chicken breasts with her chef. "Wouldn't it be wonderful to start your marriage off at someplace so beautiful?"

The front porch of Smokey Shadows Lodge offers a great view and a down-home aura.

Secret Information

Location: Maggie Valley, North Carolina.

Address: P.O. Box 444, Ski Mountain Road, Maggie Valley, North Carolina 28751.

Phone: (704) 926-0001.

Season: Year-round.

Rates: Rooms $70 a day or $360 a week; cabins $100 a day or $480 a week, June through October. Call for off-season and group rates.

Credit cards: MasterCard, Visa.

TOP SECRET

During the summer season at Smokey Shadows Lodge, owner Ginger Shinn usually serves a sumptuous, reservation-only dinner for $16.50, plus tax and tip, four nights a week. The schedule is ever changing, however, since the local businesspeople and residents who are her regulars often call and ask her to serve dinner on a night when they have guests in town. "They'll phone and say, 'Are you having dinner on Monday?' And I'll say, 'No, Tuesday,' " Shinn says. "Then they'll say, 'Oh, please open on Monday because we're having company.' So I have dinner on Monday." The menu depends on what fresh ingredients are available locally that day—for example, pork loin with just-picked apples, fresh lettuce topped with homemade dressings, native corn on the cob, squash casserole, and carrots and cabbage, followed by peach and blackberry cobbler and fresh fruit topped with ice cream. The dining room seats only forty customers (but Shinn will squeeze ten more into an adjoining room, if necessary), so call as soon as you get into town to make a reservation.

57 A Barrel of Apples

One of the surest signs that summer's over and fall has arrived is when our family gets in the van and heads to the Kyle Carver Orchard and Farm Market in Cosby, Tennessee. Although the huge warehouse is open year-round, in the autumn it's filled with a wonderful assortment of freshly picked apples and apple products. These include fresh cider and fried apple pies—slightly raised sweet dough folded over a mixture of applesauce, sugar, and cinnamon, then deep-fried to a golden brown. Yum.

Carver's, in fact, sells the largest variety of apples anywhere in the United States—130 in all. To simplify farming, harvesting, and sales to commercial distributors, most other orchards have had to specialize in just three or four kinds of apples. Carver's, however, occupying the eighty acres surrounding the farm store since 1945, has kept true to its rural agricultural roots. Unlike other farmers' markets closer to the main tourist routes (which are really disguised mini-malls), "At Carver's what you see is what you get," says Danny Carver, the owner, Kyle's grandson. "There are no gimmicks. We won't wholesale to restaurants. We don't want our products resold by others. We want customers coming back again and again. Every product is real, homemade."

Listing the apples available at Carver's at different times during the summer and fall is like repeating Bubba's rant about shrimp in *Forrest Gump*. There are McIntosh apples, Red Delicious apples, Golden Delicious apples, Granny Smith apples, Rome Beauty apples, Gala apples, Jonagold apples, Stayman Winesap apples, Arkansas Black apples, Paula Red apples, Tydeman's Red apples— well, you get the idea. Some of the varieties are older and hard to find, such as the Pippen; others are recent imports, like the Fuji, which was brought over from Japan. Because the original Carver Orchard is now

Apples, apples everywhere are the trademark of Kyle Carver Orchard and Farm Market.

part of the Great Smoky Mountains National Park—it was seized by eminent domain for a dollar an acre, much to the Carvers' continuing chagrin—the family is allowed to go into the park and take cuttings from the trees they used to own, allowing them to preserve some heritage species.

Besides apples and apple pies, the Carvers make dried fruit and apple butter (just apples, sugar, and salt cooked for up to six hours; no preservatives). They also devote some space to other people's products: locally made or grown honey, molasses, jellies, and produce such as hot peppers, beets, and nectarines.

Still, apples sold by the bushel, half bushel, bag, or tray are what Carver's is really all about. Although Danny Carver is concerned about fewer and fewer people buying big batches of fruit to put up, "The orchard is here for the long run," he says. "We don't price gouge during the tourist season, so the same customers come back again and again. The orchard business is very hard work. It is all of your life. You can't get out and there's no way to quit."

Secret Information

Location: On U.S. Highway 321, between I-40 (exit 432) and Cosby, Tennessee.
Address: 3460 Cosby Highway, Cosby, Tennessee 37722.
Phone: (423) 487-2419.
Hours: 8:00 A.M. to 6:00 P.M., every day.
Credit cards: None.

TOP SECRET

Do you know that apples sold in the supermarket look so shiny because, for better shipping, they're covered in wax, which doesn't wash off? This gives them a longer shelf life, but they also lose flavor over time. Also, you might not want to ingest indigestible wax. All the apples sold at Kyle Carver Orchard and Farm Market are tree ripened and freshly picked. Try Carver's Pippin apples, an all-purpose variety available from midwinter to midspring that's great for both eating and cooking. For the perfect pie, select a crisp Granny Smith, the Winesap, or Jonagold—all tart and firm for mouth-watering flavor and satisfying texture.

Ode to an Onion

58

Every year up to ten thousand people gather in the Smokies to pay homage to a lowly vegetable called the ramp. What exactly is a ramp, you ask? Well, it's a root bulb that's kind of like an onion but is closer to a wild leek (a garden herb of the lily family). It has tall lance-shaped leaves with a white ball at one end. It tastes a little like garlic, although it is about three times as strong. Described by old-timers as "the vilest-smelling, sweetest-tasting weed," it's said to prevent or cure colds and allergies. Health nuts bring them home only at the risk of stinking up the whole house with their pungent smell. It sounds like the perfect food to throw a party for, right? The folks of Cocke County on the eastern end of the Smokies think so. Each year on the first Sunday in May, they hold the Cosby Ramp Festival, one of the area's most diverting events.

The celebration features home-cooked foods and down-home entertainment organized by the Cosby Ruritan Club, a service organization that helps people who've had setbacks such as a house fire or who need money to attend college. To prepare for the festivities, says Carol Clark, who's married to longtime event organizer Dr. Jack Clark, "The men go into the mountains and pick the ramps that we cook during the festival." (Apparently, foraging for ramps in the forest is a guy thing.) The ostensible point of the forty-year-old festival is to honor the first vegetable available for harvest in the spring. The ramp was a fresh, vitamin-C-loaded delicacy for those Smoky settlers who had to survive the winter on unrefrigerated food. We think, however, it might just be a good excuse for a bunch of guys to get together and get their hands dirty.

The festival is held between the towns of Cosby and Newport, Tennessee, at Kineauvista Hill. People bring chairs, blankets, and coolers, then camp out all day. The foods sold are mainly ramp dishes such as scrambled eggs and ramps (the most popular way to eat ramps and a "real mess to cook," according to Clark, who has done it for years) and barbecued chicken and ramps. There are also heaping helpings of barbecued pork, beans and corn bread, fried corn bread, and other country treats. The entertainment is provided by gospel singers and other local performers. It is topped off by a beauty pageant that selects the Maid of Ramps. The winner has to eat a raw ramp. "This is a big family day. There is no wild carrying on," Clark says, summarizing the activities.

Depending on how you look at it, the Cosby Ramp Festival is an authentic slice of rural life with a family feel, or it's a bizarre hoot. Regardless, come early, grab a plate of eggs and ramps, dig in, and enjoy. Hey, what stinks around here?

Secret Information

Location: Kineauvista Hill between Newport and Cosby, Tennessee, on U.S. Highway 321.
Dates: First Sunday in May.
Prices: Admission $5 for adults; $3 for children.
For more information: Call the Newport/Cocke County Chamber of Commerce at (423) 623-7201.

TOP SECRET

If you acquire a taste for ramps while attending the Cosby Ramp Festival, you can learn how to make ramp dishes of your own by buying *Whop Biscuits and Fried Apple Pie: Cooking with Gatlinburg's Great Smoky Arts and Crafts Community* by Kathy Shields Guttman (Wordsmith Venture), a book of local recipes, including ones using ramps. It's available at shops on the Great Smoky Arts and Crafts Community loop and other local stores.

 **Helma's**

Southern Comfort Food

Speak the name *Helma* to anyone who has lived in East Tennessee more than twenty years and they'll immediately start to feel hungry. Broasted chicken, corn bread, okra, fresh green beans, cobbler, watermelon, country fried steak—Helma's Restaurant out on Asheville Highway just east of Knoxville, Tennessee, has been serving it all on one steaming buffet since 1948.

Long before "all you can eat" became an American battle cry, Helma Gilreath started her "smorgasbord" at what was then Helma's Cafe, situated in a two-pump Chevron station. When the state decided to tear down the cafe to widen the road, Helma simply built a new restaurant behind the old one. The site, at the intersection of U.S. Highway 25W to Asheville and U.S. Highway 11E to Morristown and Bristol (known as Four Way Inn to the locals because of a long-gone motel of the same name near where the roads converge), made Helma's an instant hit with travelers and truckers. Back then Interstate 40 didn't exist, so anyone traveling through these parts had to pass by Helma's, including many country music celebrities such as Tennessee Ernie Ford, Minnie Pearl, and Grandpa Jones.

"Helma cooked at her restaurant like she cooked at home," recalls daughter Jean Underwood, whose real estate office sits beside the landmark restaurant. "She'd be down at the farmers' market at 6:00 A.M. to buy fresh vegetables. When people would call and ask if she was serving fried okra that day, she would say, 'I will be by the time you get over here.' She made everyone feel like she was cooking just for them."

Helma retired and sold the restaurant in 1986 but continued to eat breakfast there until her death in 1993 at age eighty-six. "We never paid to eat there when Helma owned the restaurant, of course," Underwood recalls. "Helma was afraid that we'd forget to pay the new owners. But we never did, probably because we kept reminding each other all through breakfast."

The new owners—Jordanian-American restaurateur brothers Sam, Sami, and Nick Natour—have preserved Helma's smorgasbord format, the country-style menu items, and the restaurant itself, which looks "pretty much like it did all along," according to Underwood. The original sign advertising "curb service" and "broasted chicken in six minutes" still stands, but only table and counter service are available today and no one's timing the chickens. Even with new ownership and I-40's having taken away most of the tourist trade, Helma's remains the spot in east Knox County where home folks can find a familiar face, friendly conversation, and good food cheap.

Secret Information

Location: At the split of U.S. Highway 25W/70 and U.S. Highway 11E, east of Knoxville, Tennessee.

Address: 8606 Asheville Highway, Knoxville, Tennessee.

Phone: (423) 933-2703.

Hours: 7:00 A.M. until 8:30 P.M., Monday through Saturday; 7:00 A.M. to 8:00 P.M., Sunday.

Prices: Weekend breakfast buffet $3.75, lunch buffet $4.95, dinner buffet $5.95; Sunday buffet $6.25; menu items from $1.65 to $8.95.

Credit card: Visa.

TOP SECRET

Ask to see Helma's Blue Room, which is opened only on Sunday to accommodate the teeming after-church crowd. This back banquet room, hidden from the main dining room by a wooden partition, is somewhat of a shrine to Helma. The blue shag rug and speckled Formica-topped tables recall an earlier, tackier time. The walls are lined with photos of Helma with some of the celebrities and local dignitaries she met while operating the lucrative catering arm of her restaurant. As the first caterer in town, Helma was called upon to serve her country cooking whenever rock bands came to Knoxville or when movies and commercials were being shot in the area. Daughter Jean Underwood was given the task of buying whatever the celebrity catering clients needed from liquor to towels to a certain brand of orange juice. Recalls Underwood, "If the items on their list cost two hundred dollars, I'd charge them double that just for the pure aggravation of it all." Look for the picture of the seventies band Dr. Hook with the inscription, "To Helma—Can we have the kitchen and cooks to go?"

Cataloochee

Historic Sights

60

If the Cataloochee area in the eastern part of the Great Smoky Mountains National Park were human, it would have an inferiority complex. It would probably be jealous of all the attention Cades Cove gets for being the site of one of the earliest mountain communities. Cataloochee is just as historic, yet scads fewer visitors find their way there. Poor Cataloochee. To perk it up, we'll point out that its lack of traffic is actually a huge plus. The lack of crowds like those at Cades Cove makes it a better spot for observing how people really lived long ago.

One of five historic districts within the national park, Cataloochee's twenty-nine square miles are rich with mountain heritage. It consists of two mountain valley communities (Big Cataloochee and Little Cataloochee) separated by Noland Mountain. In the early 1900s, Cataloochee was the largest settlement in the Smokies (take that, Cades Cove), with more than two hundred buildings and a population of 1,251. Of the remaining structures in the two areas, sixteen are listed on the National Register of Historic Places. Little Cataloochee is accessible only by a two-mile hike or horseback ride.

Big Cataloochee is recommended as a scenic auto tour by Great Smoky Mountains National Park, but visitors can easily walk from building to building along the country lane. To begin your tour, be sure to stop at the Palmer House, a dog-trot-style house (named so because it has a breezeway from the front to the back porches, through which dogs can trot). Information and exhibits there will help you understand the history of the Cataloochee communities. As you walk along the back porch, imagine women and children sitting on it breaking green beans and telling stories.

After you pass the campground, you will see the Will Messer Barn, which was moved to this site from Little Cataloochee in 1977.

Cataloochee's Palmer House features a breezeway that offers a convenient dog-trot route. (Photo courtesy of Great Smoky Mountains National Park)

Then you'll come upon Palmer Chapel and Beech Grove School, white frame structures with tin roofs. Both buildings have been restored with furniture and fixtures from the past. Eighteen antique school desks are lined up in the schoolhouse, and the Methodist church even has choir pews to add to the authenticity. Across a wooden bridge is the Caldwell Place, a blue and white frame house with a wraparound porch overlooking the stream and the barn. The house is impressively paneled with wood imported from Waynesville. The road dead-ends at the beginning of Rough Fork Trail, which leads to the Woody House a mile away. Enjoy the open meadow, a playground for deer and wild turkeys and a definite photo opportunity.

Overall, Cataloochee is a wonderful walk—or drive—through the past and, except for the time it takes to get there, we think it shouldn't feel the least bit inferior to Cades Cove.

Secret Information

Location: At the eastern end of the Great Smoky Mountains National Park in North Carolina.

Season: Open all year, except when icy; campground open April through November.

Details: Allow at least three hours to explore Big Cataloochee, more if you plan to hike.

For more information, contact the Great Smoky Mountains National Park at (423) 436-1200.

TOP SECRET

Cataloochee provides standing stalls for horses and is the most popular equine camp in the Great Smoky Mountains National Park. About twenty-five hundred visitors bring their mounts from as far away as Louisiana to ride the approximately one hundred miles of trails and roads open to riders (every local route except the Boogerman Trail). Contact the national park for more information about horsing around at Cataloochee.

61

Happy Trails

Okay, so you've always dreamed of being a cowboy or cowgirl. You fantasized about ridin' the range, coolin' off with a dip in the pond, chowin' down on a steak, then kickin' back and countin' the stars. Don't give up on that yearnin'. Since 1993 K. R. "Tip" Tipton and his wife, Janice, who married at Twin Valley Bed and Breakfast and Horse Ranch's outdoor hilltop chapel, have been helping folks like you saddle up and fulfill this hankerin' for the horsey life.

The Tiptons are animal lovers, as is evident the minute you enter the gate of their 263-acre spread in Walland, Tennessee. The corral and stables are home to their thirteen steeds, a variety of breeds, from Tennessee walkers and standard breeds to appaloosas. Across the gravel driveway from the stalls lie paddocks housing a menagerie of other beasts. There guests can get together with Yukon Jack, a black and white llama, two potbellied pigs who often hide under piles of hay, a Sicilian donkey (the breed that carried Jesus into Jerusalem), and a calf who must be bottle-fed. "The kids love it," Tip says as he flashes a grin. The wild kingdom continues as you head up to the lodge along a driveway that's a playground for chickens, turkeys, bunnies, dogs, and cats.

As for people, the ranch offers a range of accommodations that allow them to mingle with plenty of other two-legged creatures, only a few, or practically none at all. The central gathering point for guests is the main lodge, which centers on a great room adorned with stuffed mallards, a boar's head, and mounted fox hides. The lived-in-looking building, which is also the Tiptons' home, features two bed-and-breakfast rooms, with private Jacuzzi baths and decorated in horse-country style. From Twin Valley's front porch, guests get a grand view of Chilhowee Mountain. Less social boarders can choose Luke's Cabin, which sleeps six and lies about a five-minute hike from the main building. Solitude seekers can opt to stay in one of two more rugged and remote primitive shelters out in the woods—four

Everything at Twin Valley Bed and Breakfast and Horse Ranch has a real rough-around-the-edges feel. (Photo by Becky Johnson)

walls, a tin roof, no bathroom facilities, and a platform on which to place sleeping bags.

A stay at Twin Valley wouldn't be complete without a guided mountain horseback ride on one of the "two-days' worth of trails." Janice, who Tip says is "boss of the horses," carefully matches the experience and comfort level of groups of six or so riders to the temperament of their mounts. She offers lessons in basic horsemanship that help even beginning riders feel comfortable in the saddle. On half-day or full-day trail rides, she describes the history of the area, tells stories about how landmarks like Hangman's Tree got their names, and identifies and explains the medicinal uses of many plants along the trail.

But horseback riding is only one of the daily activities at Twin Valley. Grab a rope and swing out over the half-acre spring-fed pond, let go, and land with a splash. Take a jaunt in a Jeep if you're staying at one of the primitive cabins and don't feel like hiking to get there. Catch a bass, trout, or catfish in the pond and let the Tiptons grill it, or join them for a campfire cookout featuring food like Tip's ribeye, barbecue chicken, hamburgers, and hot dogs. At night the animals run free and wander around the property; you might have to jump out of the way of a small herd of horses stampeding down the driveway from the lodge.

Everything at Twin Valley Bed and Breakfast and Horse Ranch has a real rough-around-the-edges feel. The Tiptons say that's just the kind of experience they want to create. Tip puts it best: "We are just down-to-earth people who enjoy meeting other down-to-earth people."

Secret Information

Location: Three miles east of U.S. Highway 321, in Walland, Tennessee.

Address: 2848 Old Chilhowee Road, Walland, Tennessee 37886.

Phone: (423) 984-0980.

Web site: www.bbonline.com/tn/twinvalley.

Rates: Lodge: $85 per night; $75 per night for three to six nights; $65 per night for seven or more nights; Luke's Cabin: $75 per night for three to six nights; $65 per night for seven or more nights; Primitive shelter: $25 per night. Horseback riding: $30 for one and a half to two hours; $50 for half day, $75 for full day. Horseback ride reservations are accepted from people not staying at the ranch. Some other activities also cost extra.

Reservations: Required.

Season: All year.

Credit cards: MasterCard, Visa.

TOP SECRET

Whether you are staying in the lodge, the cabin, or a primitive shelter at Twin Valley Bed and Breakfast and Horse Ranch, listen every morning at 8:00 A.M. for Tip's greeting from the porch of the lodge: "Good morning, World! It's a great day!" Then pay close attention as this greeting echoes through the foothills of the Great Smoky Mountains.

Old Rose and Silver Tea Room

Tea for You

62

Long before there were sex-packed paperbacks featuring Fabio on the cover, there were romance novels focused on heartfelt emotions, not on heaving bosoms and sweaty pecs.

The Danielle Steel of her day was Myrtle Reed, who wrote several turn-of-the-century parlor romances, including *Old Rose and Silver,* a favorite of Kathy Dye's and Joyce Dunavant's. "It's about a time when ladies were ladies and gentlemen were gentle," Dunavant says. "The characters have relationships, not hot flashes. They're in love, not lust."

Dye and Dunavant's yearning for simpler times inspired them to open the Old Rose and Silver Tea Room in Townsend, Tennessee. "We wanted to create the feeling of a nineteenth-century parlor," Dunavant says. "Life is so hectic in today's world. We want to promote feelings of relaxation, reflection, and not always being in such a rush." The tea room isn't intended primarily for tourists but to serve as a gathering place for the community. For example, it hosts kindergartners from nearby schools for lessons in manners.

Sitting on an upright piano at the head of the tea room is sheet music for a song called "Keep Your Eye on the Girlie You Love," and the whole place is definitely what could be called "girlie." Housed in an old brick schoolhouse, it's decorated in Victoriana and features a handful of small tables set with flowered linen and fine china. A red rose in a silver vase (neither real, unfortunately) sits on each table. The front and rear of the building are filled with antiques, crafts, and knickknacks, all of which are for sale.

The shop is open Tuesday through Saturday. Tea is served there in the afternoon three days a week. Patrons sip blends such as lavender lace and nibble on finger foods like blueberry scones and raspberry royale tea brownies. The buffet of tea and treats is tasty, if a bit pricey, but you're paying for the ambiance as much as the food and beverages. "Tea is an experience, not just a drink," Dunavant says.

The Old Rose and Silver Tea Room offers the ambiance of a nineteenth-century parlor. (Photo by Liz Duckett)

"There aren't many opportunities today for women to be women, to have tea, meet people, and just sit and chat about the day." She says that the tea room is a good place for women to escape to while the guys go hiking or fishing, although men are perfectly welcome. Some advice for the guys: Chuck the golf clubs and spend a couple hours talking over tea and treats at the Old Rose and Silver Tea Room with your significant other. Maybe the two of you will end up writing a romance novel of your own.

Secret Information

Location: On U.S. Highway 321, in Townsend, Tennessee.
Address: 7651 East Lamar Alexander Parkway, Townsend, Tennessee 37822.
Phone: (423) 448-ROSE (7673).
Hours: Antique and gift shop open 10:00 A.M. to 5:00 P.M., Tuesday through Saturday. Tea and light buffet served 1:00 P.M. to 4:00 P.M., Wednesday through Friday.
Reservations: Accepted.
Prices: $8 for afternoon tea.
Credit cards: None.

That's Kathy Dye on the left and Joyce Dunavant on the right, exhibiting the Tea Room's authentic Victorian feel. (Wade A. Payne Photography)

TOP SECRET

When visiting the Old Rose and Silver Tea Room, be sure to check out costumes worn by Kellie Martin in the television series *Christy* (Secret 16). A friend of the owners, Gayle Evans-Ivy, who now lives in Houston, designed the wardrobe for the program, and a section of the shop is set aside to display her creations. In addition, in the back of the shop, there's a room full of regularly replenished Evans-Ivy turn-of-the-century dresses for little girls and American Girl dolls for sale.

Fresh White Water

White-water rafting has always been one of the most pulse-pounding recreational options in the Smokies area. There's nothing quite like speeding down a river in a rubber raft, crashing through rapids and over small waterfalls, furiously paddling to stay on course, and silently praying that you won't pop out of the boat. It's a blast.

Until recently rafting options were limited to rivers like the Nantahala, Ocoee, and French Broad, all of which are miles away from the heart of the Smokies. Thanks to recently initiated recreational water releases from the Carolina Light and Power Plant on the Tennessee–North Carolina border, however, several outfitters have started running the Big Pigeon River. The wild water, which flows near the northern border of the Great Smoky Mountains National Park, is only a few minutes off the main thoroughfare of Interstate 40.

Several outfitters run trips on the Big Pigeon. One is Whitewater Company, founded by a group that includes Scott Strausbaugh, the only American to have won a gold medal in white-water competition at the 1992 Barcelona Olympics. They emphasize both fun and safety. It's also nice that the company offers two distinctly different white-water experiences. The Upper Pigeon trip, which puts in near Big Creek (Secret 20), features five miles of Class III and IV water, which means a roller-coaster ride over huge rocks and through rushing rapids. Limited to those aged eight and older, the trip takes about an hour and twenty minutes. Everyone—including kids, who might get tired quickly—is expected to pitch in and paddle.

For families with younger children or folks who can't stomach too much churning water or don't want to paddle as hard, the company also features a mild-water Lower Pigeon trip through Class II rapids, which is mostly flat water with one-foot waves. The only downside to choosing the Big Pigeon over other rivers is that it never strays more than one hundred yards or so from the semitruck-packed I-40, so there's not as much of a wilderness feel as on other rivers.

Secret Information

Location: Off I-40 (exit 447) in Hartford, Tennessee, near the North Carolina border.

Address: The Whitewater Company, P.O. Box 30, Hartford, Tennessee 37753.

Phone: (800) 723-8426.

E-mail: wwraft@mindspring.com.

Web site: www.mindspring.com/~snlnc/wwc.htm.

Season: Memorial Day to Labor Day.

Schedule: Three trips a day on Wednesday, Thursday, and Saturday, which are the days the dam releases water; one or two trips a day on Monday, Tuesday, and Friday; no Sunday trips. Trips go on rain or shine except when there's lightning.

Prices: $35 per person for the Upper Pigeon trip; $20 per person for the Lower Pigeon; $2 river-use fee in addition for both trips.

Credit cards: MasterCard, Visa.

Details: Expect to get drenched when rafting. The Whitewater Company, however, has changing and hot-shower facilities at its headquarters in Hartford, Tennessee.

TOP SECRET

The Big Pigeon River is the closest rafting venue to the Great Smoky Mountains National Park, but on the west side of the mountains near Cleveland, Tennessee, is the Ocoee River, site of the white-water events that were part of the 1996 Summer Olympics based further south in Atlanta. For a special splashy adventure, take a rafting ride down the Class III and IV rapids of the Olympic canoeing and kayaking course, which was constructed from 100 million pounds of rock and 8,500 cubic yards of concrete. Only recently has it been opened up to commercial outfitters, and runs are limited to a handful of days each year because of the high fees they have to pay. Check with the Ocoee White-water Visitor Center (423-496-5197), which is operated by the U.S. Forest Service, for details about dates and area outfitters.

64

Dollywood's Backdoor

It sounds simple, doesn't it? If you want to get to Pigeon Forge, Tennessee, home of Dollywood, just get off Interstate 40 at exit 407 and follow the signs. Problem is, during the busy travel days of the spring, summer, and fall, you'll likely spend the next hour or two in stops and starts as you and tens of thousands of other visitors pour through Sevierville and into the tourist town that locals call "Myrtle Beach in the Mountains."

Pigeon Forge is about a five-mile-long strip of go-cart tracks, miniature golf courses, motels, car museums, music theaters, restaurants, factory outlet stores, helicopter pads, arcades, souvenir shops—even a spot where you can skydive inside. Thanks to Dolly's decision to buy the old Silver Dollar City amusement park, the town has exploded with traffic and attractions. Even if your idea of vacation heaven is exploring the more than two hundred factory outlet stores in town, it's a hassle dealing with the hordes of other people who travel the six-lane main drag through the city.

Why waste time getting to all the fun when you can get around the congestion by taking the back way into town? About a mile and a half east of the junction of U.S. Highway 441/411 and Tennessee Highway 66 in Sevierville is Middle Creek Road. Head south on it past the hospital and travel through primarily pastureland that is more like the real feel of East Tennessee than the commercial sprawl along the main route. In about twenty minutes you'll suddenly find yourself at the back entrance to the Dollywood parking lot. Turn in and take the tram to the main entrance for a day of homespun fun without having already blown your fuse fighting traffic. Save all the hard feelings for later, when your feet hurt, you've had one too many funnel cakes, and the kids want to go on the Blazing Fury roller coaster "just one more time, *puhleez!*"

If Dollywood isn't your destination, continue on and in just a few minutes you'll come out in the heart of Pigeon Forge near a man-made waterfall at an old mill (now a restaurant) on the Little Pigeon River. You can toddle around the attractions and outlets without having had to fight all the traffic to get there, or you can head farther south to Gatlinburg and the Great Smoky Mountains National Park.

Secret Information

Secrets along the way: Blue Mountain Mist Country Inn (Secret 65) and Secrets of Dollywood (Secret 14).

TOP SECRET

Our favorite attraction in Pigeon Forge isn't a comedy barn or car museum but a place on the parkway through town called Flyaway Indoor Skydiving. Yep. It's a spot to learn how to skydive without having to jump out of a plane. For $16.92 plus tax, anyone forty pounds and up can zip into an orange jumpsuit and ride the wind in the relative safety of a powerful, padded, supervised wind tunnel. The "Flyaway Experience" consists of a thirty-minute training class, twenty-minute equipment preparation, and two-and-a-half-minute flight session. Personalized "Learn to Fly" coaching programs are also available for those wanting to learn more advanced techniques like sky boarding. For more information call (423) 453-7777.

Locator Map

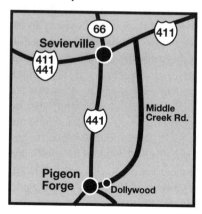

65

In the Mountain Mist

A mile and a half down winding Jay Ell Road, past the ranch and trailer homes and grazing cows, and just about when you think you've missed a turn, the earth gently dips and there on the left sits a sprawling baby blue Victorian farmhouse surrounded by sixty acres of rolling hills—the Blue Mountain Mist Country Inn. The welcoming wraparound front porch is outfitted with hammocks and rocking chairs for lazy afternoon napping or watching the sunrise (through the mist, of course) over the top of Shields Mountain.

Norman and Sarah Ball's cozy bed-and-breakfast is situated on the family's farmland, which Sarah's father, Estel Ownby, has owned for more than sixty years. Sarah grew up on the farm, became a teacher, married Norman Ball, later decided to change her career direction, and with her husband opened the Blue Mountain Mist just outside Pigeon Forge, Tennessee.

Inside the inn sweet mountain air filters through four open common rooms filled with antiques and country heirlooms. Soft mountain music plays through the CD system, and in cold weather the fireplaces crackle. An open reading room and most of the twelve uniquely decorated guest rooms are upstairs. Each has a private bath and its own distinctive touches, such as heirloom quilts, claw-foot bathtubs, or, in the Rainbow Falls Room, a stained-glass wall depicting the falls, which separates the Jacuzzi and queen-size bed. The three most expensive rooms—Rainbow Falls, LeConte Suite, and Sugarlands Bridal Room—open onto the outside balcony where you can sit and listen to the silence, broken only by cattle across the way or bullfrogs croaking in the lily pond below. If you like the bed-and-breakfast idea but want to have more privacy, there are five quaint country cottages nestled in the woods behind the inn. Each is equipped with a Jacuzzi, fireplace, kitchenette, TV and VCR, and an outdoor grill and picnic table.

The front porch of the Blue Mountain Mist Country Inn has hammocks and rocking chairs for some laid-back relaxation. (Photo courtesy of Blue Mountain Mist Country Inn)

Morning brings the sounds of nature and the ringing of a handbell calling all to a bountiful mountain breakfast featuring all the trimmings and some unexpected delights like sinfully rich stuffed French toast. As Mom used to say, come when you're called, because there's only one breakfast seating, and if you're not there on time you'll miss out.

Secret Information

Location: East of Middle Creek Road, just east of Pigeon Forge, Tennessee.

Address: 1811 Pullen Road, Sevierville, Tennessee 37862.

Phone: (800) 497-2335 or (423) 428-2335.

Rates: $85 to $130 for the inn; $140 for cottages. Off-season rates available.

E-mail: blumtnmist@aol.com.

Web site: www.bbonline.com/tn/bluemtnmist/index.htm.

Credit cards: MasterCard, Visa.

Details: Two rooms can accommodate children. There is a $15 charge for every additional person over age 1 and $5 for a child under the age of 1.

TOP SECRET

Don't let the name fool you. The Sugarlands Bridal Room at the Blue Mountain Mist Country Inn is for anyone who wants an extra-special getaway. The room is airy, open, and includes a luxurious Jacuzzi in the inn's windowed turret. The view from the bath is spectacular, but remember the balcony opens to two other rooms: Blinds might be in order when the view from the outside is something you'd rather not share.

Elderhostels

Seniors in the Smokies

Society might label seniors as over the hill, but that doesn't mean that more mature Smoky Mountains visitors aren't interested in what grows on the hill, what lives on the hill, what you can see from the hill, and how the hill got there. All that and more are covered during Elderhostel programs at the national park's week-long nature camps for those fifty-five and over.

Elderhostel is an international study program for seniors that offers courses on everything from blacksmithing to big-band music at over twelve hundred locations around the world. The Appalachian edition of the program is hosted by the Great Smoky Mountains Institute at Tremont, which offers four Elderhostel sessions a year—one in April, one in June, and two in October. Campers arrive at the facility in the western end of the Great Smoky Mountains National Park from all over the United States on a Sunday afternoon and depart the next Saturday morning. They choose from a wide range of activities that focus on subjects like photography, nocturnal wildlife, wildflower pollination, tree identification, bird identification, Cherokee history, fish of the Smokies, and astronomy. Among the special events planned by the staff at Tremont are early-morning bird watching in Cades Cove, a day-long botanical trip (during which a U.S. Forest Service manager takes campers to other areas of the Smokies to study and see different types of trees), and special sessions on how the rare red wolf has been reintroduced to the Smokies.

Campers stay at the 125-bed lodge at Tremont, men on one side and women on the other. While the sleeping arrangements don't please every married couple, "Campers rave about the good food here," the institute's Kathy Burns reports. In the evenings, learning takes a backseat to social activities as the campers prepare for barn dances and campfires. Favorites during socializing are storytelling and singing traditional tunes. In fact, Burns adds, "Most people come here for the fellowship."

A little bit of exertion and sweat goes a long way toward creating the charm of this Appalachian version of an Elderhostel. (Photo courtesy of the Great Smoky Mountains Institute at Tremont)

Secret Information

Location: Elderhostel sessions are held at the Great Smoky Mountains Institute (GSMI) in the Tremont area on the Tennessee side of the Great Smoky Mountains National Park.

Address: GSMI at Tremont, 9275 Tremont Road, Townsend, Tennessee 37882; Elderhostel, 75 Federal Street, Boston, MA 02110-1941.

Phone: GSMI at Tremont: (423) 448-6709; Elderhostel in Boston: (617) 426-8056.

Web site: GSMI at Tremont: www.nps.gov/grsm/tremont.htm; Elderhostel: www.elderhostel.org.

E-mail: GSMI at Tremont: gsmit@smoky.igc.apc.org; Elderhostel: webmstr@elderhostel.org.

Rates: $330 per person.

Credit cards: American Express, Discover, MasterCard, Visa.

Details: Each session is limited to forty campers. The program fills up fast, so register well in advance.

Elderhostel and the Great Smoky Mountains Institute at Tremont offer a hugely popular one-week-long camp each year just for grandparents and grandchildren. It's a great chance for the generations to bond while learning about the mountains. Seniors and kids ages nine to fourteen take trips into the wilderness, learn about the history of the area from guest experts, and do hands-on nature projects, among other activities. For more information, contact the GSMI at Tremont or Elderhostel.

67

Catch Your
Own Supper

This is the kind of fishing we like—no tying flies or complicated casting. No wading into freezing streams and waiting for hours for something to strike. And, best of all, no cleaning what you catch. Okay, maybe without all that we shouldn't really call it fishing. All you have to do, however, to land a delicious dinner at the Tuckaleechee Trout Farm Restaurant in Townsend, Tennessee, is grab a cane pole, put some bait on a simple metal hook on the end of a strand of nylon, and drop your line into a trout pond filled with up to three thousand rainbow trout. Most of the time, a few minutes is as long as it takes to pull in a three-quarter- to one-and-a-half-pound beauty. "It's hard to get fish that's any fresher," farm owner Larry Smith says.

The restaurant's Laurel Valley location has the reputation for the best rainbow trout in the Smokies. Smith credits this to water purified by passing through underground limestone formations en route to the stream and ponds on his property. He hatches about twenty-five thousand trout eggs a year, keeping the newborns in a separate sluice away from the adult ones, which are cannibals that like to eat their young. When the fish are properly plump, they are moved to a seventy-five-hundred-square-foot pond where diners gather round to cast their lines.

Once you catch a fish, the restaurant will clean it and serve it fried or broiled—head on or head off, it's your choice. For those who don't like the idea of meeting their meal face-to-face, they can order a fillet off the menu. Other dinner choices (we don't know why anyone would select anything but the catch of the hour, though) include steak, shrimp, and chicken. Dessert offers a delicious assortment of cobblers and pies.

Eating at Tuckaleechee is like what our friends from New England call "dining in the rough." There's absolutely no atmosphere. The restaurant is down a small dirt road that goes past a couple of trailers. The pond is a dirt-banked hole in the ground. And the dining room is like a big screened-in front porch. Smith and his wife live in a mobile home next door.

Still, folks flock to Tuckaleechee, not for the atmosphere but for the freshest fish you can find. And kids who love to play amateur angler couldn't care less about the amenities.

Secret Information

Location: About one mile east of U.S. Highway 321, just off Old Tuckaleechee Road, near Townsend, Tennessee.

Address: 142 Tipton Road, Townsend, Tennessee 37882.

Phone: (423) 448-2290.

Hours: 4:00 P.M. to 8:00 P.M., Monday through Friday; noon to 8:00 P.M., Saturday; and 2:00 P.M. to 8:00 P.M., Sunday.

Season: April through October.

Reservations: Accepted.

Prices: Entrees $4.50 to $12; dinners of catch-it-yourself trout are priced by the pound from $7.95 up (precleaned weight).

Credit cards: None.

TOP SECRET

Get your trout to go at the Tuckaleechee Trout Farm Restaurant. For four dollars a pound the restaurant will clean what you catch and pack it in ice for grilling on the balcony of your chalet or panfrying by the campfire.

Fall Foliage on the Foothills Parkway

Mountains of Color

One day we're in shorts and T-shirts trying to survive the ninety-degree temperature and the 80 percent humidity of summers in the Smokies. The next day the air will abruptly have just a whisper of a chill in it. The sky will turn from the signature haze to a bright blue. And the leaves on the trees will, one by one, start turning from green to gold, scarlet, and sienna.

Spots like Vermont are more famous for fall foliage, but we opine that the autumn colors of East Tennessee and western North Carolina are nearly as spectacular. Come fall, the mountains become covered with what looks like a big fuzzy sweater of color. Visitors come from all over the world to witness the 115 varieties of deciduous trees (those that shed their leaves as opposed to evergreens, which don't) as they react to, at first, almost imperceptible changes in sunlight and weather.

Yellows, oranges, and golds are produced by carotenes in poplars, flowering beeches, birches, buckeyes, hickories, sweet gums, and mountain ashes. Red leaves are the product of anthocyanins, which are produced by the sun and won't develop well if the fall is cloudy or too warm. They adorn red maples, dogwoods, pin cherries, sourwoods, and sumacs. Some trees in the Smokies show a mixture of colors—sugar maples, northern red oaks, and witch hobbles.

Mother Nature's biggest show in the Smokies starts in September, tends to peak during the last three weeks in October, and ends in November. During that time the most popular place to gawk at the color—the one-lane Newfound Gap road between Gatlinburg and Cherokee—oftens gets choked with foliage watchers. If you want to take a scenic drive and not spend more time watching the car in front of you than the leaves, we suggest staying outside the park proper and touring one of two segments of the Foothills Parkway, a route that was supposed to span the seventy-two miles from Cosby to Chilhowee Lake but that exists only in stops and starts.

168 ■ *100 Secrets of the Smokies*

On the east end of the Smokies area, near the Tennessee–North Carolina border, there's a short six-mile segment that stretches between I-40 and Cosby. The road reaches about twenty-three hundred feet above sea level, and there are a handful of turnoffs at which to stop and savor sweeping views of the mountains. It's a quick drive, and if you'd like to see the leaves up close, combine it with a stroll along the Cosby Nature Trail (Secret 96).

On the other end of the spectrum is the part of the parkway stretching seventeen miles from Walland, Tennessee, to the south side of the Great Smoky Mountains National Park at Chilhowee Lake. It's one of the best scenic drives because it features the peaks of the park on one side and the rolling expanse of the Tennessee Valley on the other. There are several prime spots where you can park and admire the turning of the season, but the best spot is Look Rock about midway along the road.

Secret Information

Location: The east end of the Foothills Parkway runs between I-40 (exit 443) and U.S. Highway 321, near Cosby, Tennessee. The west end stretches between U.S. Highway 321 near Walland and U.S. Highway 129 on the south side of the Great Smoky Mountains National Park.

Details: To find out when it's prime time for a foothills drive, look for the Autumn Color Report, which is posted locally at the Sugarlands Visitor Center and other area tourist information spots. To get fall foliage information by phone, call Sugarlands at (423) 436-1291.

TOP SECRET

As you drive the Walland–Chilhowee Lake leg of the Foothills Parkway, you'll see a turnoff for the Top of the World community. This enclave is a collection of vacation homes on a private lake perched on the top of a mountain. Although you can't use the lake, the community is worth a quick detour, and you can stop at the local chapel for a few moments to admire the autumn peace and quiet of one of the most truly secluded and secret spots in the Smokies.

69

Quilt Trip

A basic handmade quilt costs $685 at Holloway's Country Home store in Cosby, Tennessee. Sound expensive? Believe it or not, that's a bargain. Store owner Maria Holloway points out that hand sewing the colorful patterns of authentic Appalachian quilts takes a minimum of three hundred hours. If a quilter earned just the minimum wage of $5.15 an hour, a basic quilt would cost $1,545, before any equipment, materials, or markup. So $700 is really a steal.

"Quilting is done for the love of it, not for the money," Holloway says. She adds that old-time quilters are dying out or losing their eyesight, and few young people are learning the craft. She predicts that the price of authentic quilts, as opposed to those that are machine manufactured, will soon soar as fewer and fewer new ones are created.

If you can't afford the price of a new quilt, don't let that put you off from visiting Holloway's out-of-the-way country store. Actually, the place is more like a home. It consists of a building built in the 1700s that was moved to Cosby from Jonesboro, the second story from another historic building, and a newer structure connecting the two. Inside it's stuffed with crafts, fabrics, furniture, and artwork, such as slate shingles salvaged from old roofs and then painted with flowers and other decorations. Quilts cost up to seventy-eight hundred dollars, but there are plenty of items for those of us of more modest means. Antique quilts, for example, start at three hundred dollars and you can try making your own quilt by buying kits that cost between $14.95 and $155.

Holloway's grandmother was a quilter, and the native New Englander got interested in sewing and creating colorful designs as a child. In 1981, she moved to Gatlinburg, started creating her own quilts, and opened a place to sell them. Over the years that shop became too small, and she moved to the current property in Cosby.

Business boomed, and Holloway opened a satellite shop in the Morning Mist Galley mall in the Great Smoky Arts and Crafts Community (Secret 90). Holloway, now a grandmother of three, still designs and lays out each quilt, although she doesn't do the sewing.

Holloway says the store tends to attract middle-aged people and seniors who are "true connoisseurs of American art." Some customers send in special orders accompanied by a swatch of wallpaper or fabric and ask her to design the perfect quilt to match a particular room's decor.

Secret Information

Location: On U.S. Highway 321, in Cosby, Tennessee.
Address: 3892 Cosby Highway, Cosby, Tennessee 37222.
Phone: (423) 487-3866.
Hours: 9:00 A.M. to 5:00 P.M., every day, although call ahead on Sunday because Holloway and her staff may have decided to take the day off. The store is closed from December 20 to January 20.
Credit cards: Discover, MasterCard, Visa.

TOP SECRET

At the back of the Holloway's Country Home property is Maria's Country Closet and Sewing Room, used exclusively for making the hand-sewn clothes for women, girls, and dolls sold upstairs in the main store. Prices range from a few dollars to several hundred. The styles are basically country dresses, jackets, and cloaks—many are quilt-style collections of fabric pieced together. Stop in at the back building if you want to place a custom clothing order—special requests take priority over other projects because they're already paid for.

70

Down by the River

Spanning the French Broad River right near the Jefferson-Sevier county line in Tennessee stands one of the Tennessee Valley Authority's crown jewels. Constructed during the agency's World War II heyday, it's the concrete behemoth called Douglas Dam. It was built for flood prevention and hydroelectric production, which are essential for local residents but rather inconsequential to vacationers. What you do need to know (as many locals already do), however, is that situated along the tree-lined riverbank below the dam is one of the cleanest, quietest campgrounds in the area.

Now, if you head out to the dam and start looking for camping signs, you'll never find Douglas Dam River Campground. The TVA knows it's there. The locals know it's there. So why put up a sign? There is a blue and white TVA sign that reads "River Recreation and Powerhouse." Apparently, part of the "river recreation" is camping, because if you follow the road down to the river, there is a small camping sign directing you to the right. Simply finding the camp area makes you feel kind of special. Tenting out under the stars on a riverbank site makes you feel even better.

Douglas Dam River Campground is operated by the TVA. That one fact weeds out all of the yahoos you might expect to find at a riverside campground in Tennessee. TVA security monitors the single-road facility and sets the rules, which include no alcohol and no wild parties. The rest room/shower buildings are fairly new and sparkle as bright as any residential bathroom. There are plenty of trash receptacles—all emptied regularly—and well-maintained picnic tables and grills are at each first-come, first-served site.

The Douglas Dam River Campground is good for lots of things like biking and roller-blading on the paved, traffic-free road that runs the length of the campground. But as tempting as the cool French Broad River looks from your riverbank perch, swimming in the camp

A campground that offers tent sites with a great view of a dam is one thing; another is a campground that bans alcohol and wild parties. This makes Douglas Dam River Campground a nice spot for families.

area is not recommended. As any white-water aficionado will tell you, the water just below a dam provides some ragin' rapids when there's a release. That means the current on the section of the river that runs through the campground is unpredictable and dangerous. Although you can venture into the river with a personal flotation device, most campers hike, bike, or drive over to the milder, Douglas Lake side of the dam to swim. There's also a nice TVA campground on the lake side, but it's not as secluded or as serene as the river site. In addition, the Douglas Dam Lake Campground is where most local boaters put in their pontoons, fishing boats, and jet skis; so the parking lot can be pretty busy on weekends and a bit dicey for camper kids on roller blades or bikes.

The rapid river water at the river campground is perfect for freshwater fishing, however, which is the sport of choice for most campers. If you didn't pack a pole, the TVA-operated Douglas Canteen at the campground entrance stocks cane poles with line for $4.95 and rods with reel and line for $19.95. They also sell live bait, tackle, fishing licenses, and fire logs for cooking your catch at the end of the day. In addition, the canteen has outdoor soda and ice machines, a pay phone and rest rooms, plus a little grocery stocked with camping essentials such as bug spray, milk, and junk food.

The land directly across the river from the campground is TVA-owned, too, and uninhabited except for blue herons, butterflies, and wildflowers. The lack of nearby human neighbors keeps the river area quiet and dark at night, perfect for stargazing, lightning bug watching, or simply settling down in your sleeping bag for a restful night's sleep. If you're up for a little more action, there's usually a kickball or touch football game available on the grassy playing field or a volleyball game at the campground's grass court. If that's too tame, then the bright lights of Sevierville and Pigeon Forge are only a few minutes away, which is hard to believe when you're surrounded by water, woods, and welcome silence.

Secret Information

Location: On the northwest side of Douglas Dam off Tennessee Highway 139, north of Sevierville, Tennessee.

Address: Douglas Dam River Recreation area, Sevierville, Tennessee 37725.

Phone: The Douglas Canteen number is (423) 453-9683.

Prices: $15 per day for sites with electricity; $11 for those without, paid at the self-service station.

Details: You can occupy the same site for up to twenty-one days. All sites have water, a grill, and a picnic table.

TOP SECRET

A short bike ride, hike, or drive up the road from Douglas Dam River Campground lies the Douglas Dam Overlook. Even if you don't care about seeing the dam, the panoramic view of Douglas Lake and the Smokies is magnificent from way up here. There are two overlooks—one right on top of the dam and the other up a paved drive to the crest of a grassy hill. Check out the lower spot first for an up-close-and-personal view, then climb or drive up the hill for the sweeping vista. The hilltop visitor center also offers plenty of picnic tables and clean rest rooms. With acres of manicured lawn for the kids to romp and roll on, the Douglas Dam Overlook is the perfect spot for a picnic, regardless of whether you're camping at the dam or not. And since it's off the beaten tourist path and is usually fairly empty, especially during midweek, the overlook is the ideal place to lie on the grass and read or to snooze away a summer afternoon.

71

Wild Wildlife

More than ten million people visit the Great Smoky Mountains National Park every year, but even that huge population of people is a minority when you look at life in the park. Even if you can't always see it, wildlife is everywhere amid the area's more than eight hundred square miles of wilderness. The diverse animal population includes some fifty-eight species of mammals, sixty species of fish, more than two hundred species of birds, twenty-three of snakes, twenty-nine of salamanders, seventy-five of butterflies, and thousands of other species of insects.

Still, the woods aren't quite the same as they were when only the Cherokee roamed the perimeter up to the early and mid-1700s. When the white settlers began flowing into the area, the gray wolf, river otter, and mountain lion lived there but soon succumbed to intense hunting and trapping. Clear-cutting the land invited white-tailed deer to move in, and they still flourish in places like Cades Cove. The raccoons, black bears, and foxes were also hunted intensively, but each managed to survive as a species. About six hundred of the beloved black bears inhabit the park, probably the highest number there has ever been in the twentieth century.

Bears are the most-sought-after wildlife to see in the park. Standing about three feet tall, and weighing anywhere from 125 to 400 pounds, they're what you call "opportunistic feeders." They make lunch of just about any available food, including berries, nuts, insects, ants, grubs, plants, small animals, fish, and even carrion. They are nonaggressive, but remember that they can climb trees, and large bears can reach up nearly nine feet without jumping. To avoid close encounters of the furry kind, store food in the car or hang it at least twelve feet above the ground from the lines and poles provided at some bear-prone campsites. Black bears can

Owls help keep the watch in the Smokies. (Photo courtesy of Great Smoky Mountains National Park)

sometimes be spotted in Cades Cove or in other open areas, scavenging for food in the evenings and early mornings.

The Smokies are also a mecca for bird-watching enthusiasts, who come to see both residents and migraters. Warblers galore, including the chestnut-sided and black-throated green warblers, scarlet tanagers, ravens, pileated woodpeckers, whippoorwills, nighthawks, owls, and more can be found here, depending on season, elevation, and terrain.

Far less loved is the wild boar, an exotic pest animal that proliferates like a rabbit and roots like the hog that it is. Originally a European, it was imported to this country in 1912 and brought to a private hunting preserve in North Carolina. There might be as many as one thousand boars now in the park. For much of the year, the wild boar lives on mast—mostly nuts. To find the food, boars root freely in the soil, destroying plants and soil. The rest of the time, they root for other things—wildflower bulbs and roots, salamanders, beetles—all of which also live in or close to the soil. The park has eradication programs aimed directly at this animal.

A specialty of the Smokies is the salamander. Nowhere else outside the tropics are salamanders so plentiful and so diverse. Biologists are still counting and reclassifying them. The redcheek salamander, common above thirty-five hundred feet, is found nowhere else in the world except the park. Nocturnal, as are all salamanders, they spend their days conserving skin moisture underneath rocks, logs, and beneath the bark of downed trees.

Of the zillions of insects, many of which have undoubtedly never been classified, the scorpion and hanging flies are some of the most interesting. So named because the males have a bulbous protrusion on their abdomen resembling that of a scorpion, the scorpion fly is no threat to humans. The hanging flies hang from their front legs and catch insects with the tips of their hind legs.

Secret Information

For more information about wildlife in the Smokies, we suggest *Birds of the Smokies* (Great Smoky Mountains Natural History Association) and *Trees of the Smokies* by Steve Kemp (Great Smoky Mountains Natural History Association). School-aged children will also love a storybook by local artist and writer Lisa Horstman that features some of the Smokies' slimy residents; it's called *The Great Smoky Mountain Salamander Ball* (Great Smoky Mountains Natural History Association).

TOP SECRET

The Wilderness Wildlife Week is an annual event held during the last week in January at the Heartlander Country Resort in Pigeon Forge near the Great Smoky Mountains National Park. Days are packed with informative classes, taught by experts, covering a gamut of such topics as bald eagle releases and wildlife photography. Guided bird-watching hikes are also part of the program. Better yet, the entire event is free. For more information call the Pigeon Forge Department of Tourism at (423) 453-8574 or (800) 251-9100.

Bed and Repast

72

Vincent and Sharlene Barrington were hunting for the perfect place in East Tennessee to open their dream bed-and-breakfast. He's from England, lived for a bit in South Africa, and met Sharlene, an Ohio native, when he moved to Florida. Over two decades the pair have shared adventures such as rebuilding a forty-foot sailboat and spending two years living on it cruising the Caribbean and then opening the Iguana Restaurant in Key West. On a trip north to visit friends who had moved from Florida, they fell in love with the Smokies. They later returned to the area and spent a week with a real estate agent looking for the right property. No luck. Then their realtor reluctantly told them that he had one last place to show, but added that they wouldn't want to buy it. He took them to a twenty-four-acre dairy farm just off I-40 in New Market, Tennessee, which centered on a rundown farmhouse that hadn't been lived in for twenty years. After touring the property for ten minutes and imagining what they could create there, they told the shocked agent, "We'll take it."

"We haven't regretted it for a minute," Vince says. The couple spent four years renovating and expanding the house, originally a pre-Civil War log cabin. The result is a hospitable three-story white frame farmhouse set amidst towering maple trees, a nearby barn, and a natural spring.

Frankly, we aren't sure whether to recommend the Barrington as a great place to stay or as a great place to eat—it's both. It's one of the few bed-and-breakfasts that's also a gourmet restaurant open to nonguests. As a place to stay, it's a quiet retreat, just two and a half miles on the north side of I-40, a world away from all the hustle and bustle of tourist traffic on the south side, yet close enough to anything you might want to do in the mountains.

Assisted by their daughter Dianne, the Barringtons do everything possible to make guests feel at home in their home. Their living

The Barrington Inn and Restaurant represents a dream come true for its owners.

room, a sunken great room featuring a floor-to-ceiling stone fireplace, is shared openly with guests. The seven bedrooms—four in the main house and three in a recently completed annex that was once a milking building—are decorated with touches from the couple's past. One room, for example, boasts a South African theme—native masks, a machete, a watercolor of an African market theme. Another, with a more English flair, is adorned with a green and mauve scheme, Chippendale furniture, and a teddy bear perched on the bed. "At the Barrington Inn, you never know where you'll find a bear," Sharlene likes to joke.

Equally enticing is the food. Vincent, who once cooked aboard tankers and cruise ships, concocts all the meals, including stomach-stuffing breakfasts (included in the room rate) of items like French toast smothered in stewed apples, maple syrup, and whipped cream. The Barrington is also open to guests and the public alike for dinner from Thursday through Saturday. In a dining room that centers on back-to-back fireplaces, the Barringtons serve such items as escargots in mushroom caps, alligator chowder, New Zealand grilled lamb chops, lobster and shrimp croustade, and, for dessert, crème brûleé. "Dinners are exciting," Sharlene says.

"Vincent is known for his sauces and he learned many recipes as he traveled over most of the world." Some of the ingredients come directly from a vegetable garden and more than thirty fruit trees on the property.

Secret Information

Location:	Just north of I-40 (exit 412), west of Dandridge, Tennessee.
Address:	1174 McGuire Road, New Market, Tennessee 37820.
Phone:	(423) 397-3368 or (888) 205-8482.
Season:	All year, although the Barringtons sometimes close for their vacation.
Room rates:	$85 to $100 (includes breakfast).
Restaurant hours:	5:00 P.M. until "everyone is served," Thursday through Saturday.
Restaurant prices:	Entrees $9.95 to $20.95.
Restaurant reservations:	Required.
Credit cards:	Discover, MasterCard, Visa.
Details:	Bring your own wine and the staff will serve it for a small set-up fee. Dress for dinner is country-club casual.

TOP SECRET

Guests who stay at the Barrington Inn get a 20 percent discount on the price of dinner. Our favorite is the lobster and shrimp croustade, seafood cooked in a puff pastry that Vince Barrington carefully sculptures into the shape of a lobster.

73

**Jubilee Community Arts
at the Laurel Theater**

Come to the
Jubilee

The Pigeon Forge, Tennessee, area is becoming a little like Branson, Missouri, with its numerous and mammoth new music theaters featuring star performers like Lee Greenwood. These shows are flashy and fun, but to sample authentic Appalachian sounds and a more diverse menu of melodies, bypass the music mansions and head on over to Knoxville's historic Fort Sanders neighborhood, home of Jubilee Community Arts at the Laurel Theater.

Jubilee is a nonprofit group dedicated to promoting, preserving, and protecting the traditional art and artisans indigenous to southern Appalachia. The group is headquartered at the Laurel Theater—a converted 1895 Presbyterian church, listed on the National Register of Historic Places and sitting smack-dab in the middle of Big Orange Country: the University of Tennessee campus. Throughout the year the Laurel hosts a sampling of the region's native performers, with the emphasis on traditional string bands, ballad singers, and storytellers. Laurel favorites include the area's best bluegrass, folk, and alternative musicians, like the banjo-pickin', fiddle playin', toe-tappin' Hominy Mamas.

Then there are the southern Appalachian storytellers such as Lloyd Arneach, a Native American born and raised on the North Carolina Cherokee reservation, who shares legends and folktales about his people and other tribes. The church's original cathedral ceilings and massive stained-glass window (its matching window was broken and has been replaced with a clear pane that lets in a view of the trees and sunlight), combined with the sweet sounds of a dulcimer, fiddle, banjo, bongo, or guitar make the Laurel Theater the perfect spot to spend a truly Appalachian summer afternoon or evening.

"Anybody who is anyone in terms of folk and traditional music has played at the Laurel," longtime Jubilee board member Lou Gross says. "Doc Watson and Alison Krauss have played here, and John McCutcheon performed his very first public concert with Jubilee."

The traditional southern Appalachian arts presented at the Laurel aren't confined to the English and Scottish traditions normally associated with the mountain region, however. Although few people realize it, East Tennessee has long-established African American, Indian (of the continent), Palestinian, and Jewish communities, and an emerging Bosnian-refugee population whose rich heritages are all celebrated by Jubilee. Says Brent Cantrell, the Jubilee's latest executive director: "Part of our mission is to present and promote the various art forms and traditions of all of the peoples who have settled in this region."

Every June, Jubilee produces the International Jubilee Festival at Knoxville's World's Fair Park. This one-day extravaganza features the food, music, dance, and other art forms of the region's various cultures. "It is great seeing people dressed in their different native home dress talking and celebrating with each other," Cantrell says. Huge plates of international fare found at the eclectic food court cost under four dollars, and free cooking demonstrations are presented throughout the day.

Secret Information

Location: Near the University of Tennessee campus in Knoxville, Tennessee.
Address: 1538 Laurel Avenue, Knoxville, Tennessee 37916.
Phone: (423) 522-5386 or (423) 522-5851.
Web site: funnelweb.utcc.utk.edu/~tkoosman/jca.
Details: Call for upcoming concert information.

TOP SECRET

On Wednesdays and Thursdays during the summer, the staff of the Jubilee Community Arts at the Laurel Theater clear away all the benches, throws blankets and quilts on the theater's glossy hardwood floors, and welcomes families and day-care groups for the popular Children's Jubilee Concert Series. The 10:30 A.M. shows are geared toward seven-year-olds and younger, and the 1:00 P.M. shows are designed for the more sophisticated eight-and-up crowd. Such performers as female folk/rock duo Wishing Chair, a sort of Indigo Girls for kids, delight their pint-size audiences with an interactive sing-along. The two dollars per ticket (kids under two are free) is way cheaper than an hour at an arcade or minigolf.

74

Roads Less Traveled

Back in the 1920s folks around here had a bright idea: Create a scenic highway, like the Blue Ridge Parkway and the Natchez Trace, that would span the foothills of the Smokies and feature the most spectacular views of the area's mountains. Well, it took until 1944 for Congress to finally provide the initial funding for the seventy-two miles of pavement stretching from Snow Mountain on the north side of the national park to Chilhowee Lake on the south side, then another sixteen years for construction to finally begin in 1960. Now, nearly forty years later, only 22.5 miles have been completed.

The rest of the road is in limbo, including an eighteen-mile section between Wears Valley and Walland, Tennessee, that was started in the early 1980s. Two contractors were hired to work from opposite ends of the segment and they completed everything except the paving on two spurs that were supposed to meet in the middle of the mountains. Unfortunately, the government neglected to contract for a particularly difficult stretch of construction in Caylor Gap, causing the two roads to come to an abrupt halt in the wilderness—1.6 miles short of each other.

"We call that the 'missing link,'" says Dean Stone, past president of the Foothills Parkway Association. The group was formed a few years ago to speed up the process of finishing the parkway by raising money and pushing for more federal funding. The estimated cost of finishing just the Wears Valley–Walland stretch is $56 million. "The prettiest views of the Smokies are in the section of the foothills between Walland and Wears Valley," says Stone, who has edited the *Blount County Daily Times* for more than fifty years. "You can't imagine how beautiful the mountains are until you've seen them from that point of view."

The orphaned sections are closed to motor vehicles, but open to hikers, bikers, and horseback riders. Because they are wide, packed with fine gravel, and graded to rise slowly, they are relatively easy to walk or bike for folks who aren't that fit. The eastern spur that starts in Wears Valley is only four miles long and rises about one thousand feet from bottom to top. The western section, which starts in Walland, is nine miles long and is the more scenic of the two sections because it overlooks the relatively undeveloped Tuckaleechee Cove area.

Secret Information

Location: The unfinished Walland spur of the Foothills Parkway starts at the entrance to the finished Walland–Chilhowee Lake section that starts off Highway 321 (Secret 55) about twelve miles south of Maryville. Take the Foothills Parkway turnoff, but rather than heading right to Chilhowee Lake, turn left and park at the gate blocking the start of the unfinished portion. The Wears Valley spur starts on Highway 321 about twelve miles from Townsend and twenty-nine miles from Pigeon Forge. Look for the only overpass in the valley and park in the gravel area near the road's entrance.

TOP SECRET

For two weekends a year the Foothills Parkway Association opens the unfinished spurs of the Foothills Parkway to automobile traffic and solicits donations toward completing construction of the road. The April open house, usually the fourth weekend of the month, is timed to feature redbuds and dogwoods in full bloom. The October opening, generally the third weekend (unless there's a University of Tennessee home football game), is timed to coincide with the peak of fall foliage. Call the Great Smoky Mountains National Park at (423) 436-1200 a few weeks in advance to find out the specific dates when the roads will be open.

75

Lessons from the Past

Whenever our children complain about how hard school is, we remind them that they could have attended the Little Greenbrier School, just inside the Great Smoky Mountains National Park near the Metcalf Bottoms Campground in Tennessee. The one-room schoolhouse was built in 1882 and used for instruction (and for church on Sundays) until 1935, about the time the national park was established.

The wooden building is perched a short drive up a dirt road in a clearing edged with split-rail fences. Inside it's dark, with four narrow windows providing only limited light. Facing the blackboard at the front of the room are rows of seats, although when the school was in use the children sat on benches, taller ones for bigger children and shorter ones for the smaller ones. For eight hours a day boys sat on one side of the room, girls on the other. Everyone brought whatever books they had—a math book, a spelling book—and shared with one another. They carried their lunches to school in white oak baskets and tin buckets that had once held lard. Most midday meals consisted of leftovers from the previous night's supper. Students wrote on slates and wiped them clean with shirt sleeves. They played with dolls made out of wooden spoons, socks, and gourds. Some school sessions lasted only six weeks while others lasted eight months. In the winter the schoolroom was heated only by an old-fashioned cookstove.

Retired teacher Elsie Burrell until recently conducted school each Tuesday to show park visitors what it was like to attend Greenbrier. Dressed as a stern schoolmarm in a long skirt with a white apron, a blue and white buttoned-down blouse, red, white, and blue quilted vest, dark stockings, dark comfortable-looking shoes, and an orchid and white gingham bonnet embroidered with a purple iris (the Tennessee state flower), she would conduct lessons that included an old-fashioned spelling bee. Cool nineties kids in Nikes

The Greenbrier School was built in 1882. Retired teacher Elsie Burrell, pictured here, until recently conducted classes for visitors one day a week. (Photo courtesy of Great Smoky Mountains National Park)

soon discovered that children in the 1890s had it much harder. Burrell demonstrated the old-school way by ordering "students" to sit down because they didn't follow orders "to pronounce the word, spell it, and pronounce it again." Sadly, Miss Elsie, who is in her nineties, broke her hip and had to retire from her role, but the park has promised equally interesting new programs in her place.

With or without a teacher, visiting Little Greenbrier School is a fascinating trip back into the past. After every visit we have made with our family, our children don't complain much about school at all.

Secret Information

Location: Near the Metcalf Bottoms Campground, which is just off Little River Road, on the Tennessee side of the Great Smoky Mountains National Park.

This view inside the one-classroom Greenbrier School shows rows of seats, although students actually sat on benches when school was in session between 1882 and 1935. (Photo courtesy of Great Smoky Mountains National Park)

TOP SECRET

Some students walked as far as nine miles a day, each way, to attend Little Greenbrier School. To get an idea of what that was like, after touring the school, hike the mile or so to the still-standing cabin that the Walker sisters, who attended Little Greenbrier, lived in. Charts on the wall of the school show the genealogy of the Walker family. After the sisters were interviewed in 1946 by *The Saturday Evening Post*, the park service posted a sign on Highway 73 directing curious tourists to the sisters' cabin. The sisters decided to cash in a bit on all the attention (and aggravation) by making mountain souvenirs to sell to the flatlanders. But in 1953, when only two sisters remained, Margaret Jane and Louisa wrote to the park superintendent requesting that the "sign 'bout the Walker sisters" be taken down. Their reason for the request? "We're 70 and 82 and can't make sovioners [*sic*] to sell and the people will be expecting them."

Creekside Camping

76

"Most people find us by luck," says Butch Shermer, the young, amiable outdoor enthusiast, who, along with his wife, Mary, own Moonshine Creek Campground Resort. "And once they find us they keep coming back."

Shermer says most of his clients are either satisfied customers who return annually or their friends checking out Moonshine Creek for themselves. Because of Moonshine's secluded location, few campers stumble upon the twenty-six-acre enclave in western North Carolina. Although Moonshine Creek is only a half-mile south of the Blue Ridge Parkway and a couple of miles off U.S. Highway 23/74, the back roads to get there are full of twists and turns—the last little bit on tire-testing gravel. Even when following the resort's signs, you might be tempted to give up and turn around along the way, but forge ahead. It's worth the bumpy ride.

"If you're looking for lots of noise and a parking-lot layout and need to be right on the highway, then we're not for you," says Shermer, who prides himself in offering what he terms "positively outrageous service" to his customers. "We offer a secluded setting for people who want to be in the wilderness. While they're here, we spoil the heck out of 'em by taking them personally to their site and bringing out wood and ice."

The twenty primitive camping sites (no hookups), fifty-nine campsites (full hookups), and seven camping cabins are hidden in the trees on either side of babbling Moonshine Creek. The sound of the clear mountain water is soothing, but Shermer has had some requests from city folks to "shut the water off" at night. The moonshine still, for which the campground was named, is on display at the campground and was reportedly used until the seventies.

At thirty-two hundred feet above sea level and blanketed by a canopy of trees, the campground offers cool comfort all summer long. "We're near the Blue Ridge Parkway and the Smokies, but

Surely you didn't think that Moonshine Creek Campground would be complete without some moonshine stills?

many people never leave once they arrive," says Shermer, "because if you come to the mountains to be in the mountains and surrounded by peace and quiet and nature, then you've found it here." Shermer knows the backroads and secret haunts of the area and shares them freely with his guests. Once you arrive he'll help plan whatever itinerary you desire, such as peace, wilderness adventure, or sightseeing.

Although Moonshine Creek offers occasional weekend and holiday campfires, cookouts, and sing-alongs, this is not a place for parents who want to "drop their kids," Shermer says. Instead of daily organized activities, Moonshine Creek offers families opportunities to spend time together hiking, roasting marshmallows, and catching their own trout for supper in a nearby stocked pond. There's also badminton, Ping-Pong, darts, an exercise bike, and a lend/swap library; but the main focus is firmly on the outdoors that envelop the campground. "We had one couple who liked it here so much they're building a home just down the road," says Shermer. "It would be hard to find a prettier place in the Smokies than right here."

Secret Information

Location: Off U.S. Highway 23/74 in Balsam, south of Waynesville, North Carolina.

Address: Box 10, Dark Ridge Road, Balsam, North Carolina 28707.

Phone: (704) 586-6666.

Rates: Tent/full-hookup RV site $14 to $18; camping cabin $27 to $32; furnished rental $41 to $43 (three-night minimum).

Season: April 1 through November 1.

Credit cards: MasterCard, Visa.

TOP SECRET

The most-sought-after camping spot at Moonshine Creek Campground Resort is site 58. The waterfall runs behind the site and its location at the very back of the campground makes it the most secluded.

77

Where Everybody Knows Your Name

At the end of a shady road that winds up a hill just outside Gatlinburg, Tennessee, lies the Greenbrier Restaurant. Coming upon it, you can almost imagine the days in which the hunting lodge was built by George Dempster, Knoxville's mayor at the time. He and his sisters owned over two hundred acres in the area, much of which today is a part of the Great Smoky Mountains National Park. Dempster, like other members of the upper class, enjoyed escaping the city, such as it was sixty years ago, and spending time in what was then the remote village of Gatlinburg, high in the mountains.

Few reminders of those days remain, but the large log-cabin-like lodge still stands. It's another kind of rustic retreat—a favorite spot for locals to gather away from the hordes of visitors who clog the main parts of town. As restaurant manager and chef David Hadden describes it, "It is the real Gatlinburg, out of the way, not fast paced like downtown. Everybody knows everybody."

One time in the early eighties David's parents, Dean and Barbara Hadden of Pompano Beach, Florida, were on their way to North Carolina, when they stopped over in Gatlinburg. They fell in love with the Greenbrier property, bought it, and stayed. Dean, who had been in the restaurant business all his life and who taught son David how to cook and how to run a food operation, was the gourmet chef and proprietor, while Barbara kept the books and handled the business. Dean died in 1991, and Barbara, who is still the owner, works from home, while son David and daughter-in-law Becky manage the restaurant.

The Greenbrier has received the prestigious People's Choice Award for Fine Dining. Becky boasts that the specialty of the house is the slow-cooked prime rib, which is so popular that they sometimes run out of it. Close seconds in popularity are the Smoky Mountains strip steak, marinated in garlic and olive oil for

The Greenbrier
Restaurant occupies
a rustic lodge with a
log-cabin feel.
(Photo by Liz Duckett)

a couple of days, and chicken Vera Cruz, a whole chicken breast stuffed with a crabmeat dressing and provolone cheese and topped with a white wine sauce. There also are locally grown mountain trout, sumptuous stuffed pork tenderloin medallions, and a filet and lobster combination.

In recent years the Haddens have upgraded the restaurant by adding an entry patio and a spacious step-down dining room that seats seventy-five and features an emerald woodland view through floor-to-ceiling windows. Fireplaces throughout the building warm the winter evenings. In contrast to the serene dignity of the dining area, the cozy six-stool bar and cocktail lounge is a blaze of orange and white University of Tennessee football decorations.

Although casually elegant, the Greenbrier has a welcoming family feel. A couple of well-filled photo albums of staff and customers are kept in the lobby, and everyone is invited to pore through them. So close are the local patrons and the restaurant's staff that one day each spring the restaurant is closed for a family picnic. And should Becky, the bar manager, ever need to run to town, she'll tell her regulars, "Watch the bar," and she knows it will be safe until her return.

Secret Information

Location: Off U.S. Highway 321, just east of downtown Gatlinburg, Tennessee.

Address: 370 Newman Road, Gatlinburg, Tennessee 37738.

Phone: (423) 436-6318.

Hours: 5:00 P.M. to 10:00 P.M., April through December; 4:30 P.M. to 9:30 P.M., January through March.

Reservations: Not accepted.

Prices: Entrees $12.95 and up; children's menu available.

Credit cards: American Express, Diners Club, Discover, MasterCard, Visa.

TOP SECRET

One recent Monday, Jordan Hadden, then six, started yelling, "*Dad! Daddy! Dad!!!* There was a girl standing beside me, and I tried to get you to turn around . . . but now she's gone!" His mother, Greenbrier Restaurant bar manager Becky Hadden, says her son, who knew none of the history of the Greenbrier, might have seen the ghost of "the Jilted Lady," Lydia. The story goes that sometime in the late twenties, the sweet, raven-haired beauty who lived in the old lodge was left at the altar. In despair, she returned home unwed and hanged herself from the rafters. Two days later, the mauled body of her lover was found in the mountains. Legend says Lydia transformed into a mountain cat and took her revenge. Since that time many have reported seeing her. One lodge caretaker was terrified by her cries, "Mark my grave! Mark my grave!" After he placed a cross of twigs on her resting place, her pleas were heard no more, yet her silent form is said to wander the Greenbrier Restaurant to this day.

Cherokee Nation

Cherokee, North Carolina, is the main gateway to the south side of the Great Smoky Mountains National Park. It's the commercial center of what is known as the Qualla Boundary, the home of the eastern band of the tribe that was split by the forced march along the Trail of Tears in the 1830s. Because U.S. Highway 441/Newfound Gap Road, the main route through the national park between Tennessee and North Carolina, deposits millions of tourists there, the town is the first and most lasting impression visitors get of this proud and culturally rich Native American nation.

That's unfortunate. For the most part, Cherokee is Pigeon Forge with colored feathers. Shop after junky shop sells rubber-bladed hatchets, bright-colored headdresses, and brown-skinned plastic Indian dolls made in China. Outside many stores are braves in full war paint and headdress—Cherokee men with names like Killing Bear and Painted Horse—who will pose for pictures for three to five dollars, if you bring your own camera. Some stand in front of metal or buckskin teepees, while others are accompanied by long-dead bears whose stuffed skin is balding in spots. A few of the bears and mannequin braves are even mounted on wheeled platforms, so they can be pulled out in front in the morning and back inside at night. Other not-so-native attractions include the new Harrah's casino, which has joined Tribal Bingo and Tribal Casino as twenty-four-hour-a-day, seven-day-a-week operations that employ hundreds of reservation residents and keep the streets congested with bumper-to-bumper traffic. We're not opposed to people making a buck or two to help the local economy, but downtown Cherokee is not an attractive portrait of Native American culture.

If you're coming from Tennessee and want to avoid the typical logjam of cars, there are a couple options. First, to skip downtown Cherokee altogether but still see part of the reservation, the majority of which isn't at all that touristy, take a left onto the Blue Ridge Parkway just after the Oconaluftee Visitor Center. This section of the parkway takes you through a few tunnels and offers spectacular overlooks, including one at mile marker 459 of the Qualla Indian Reservation. Seeing the reservation from above is far more picturesque and much less stressful than battling the traffic on 441. Stay on the Blue Ridge for fourteen miles to the first exit—Route 19/Cherokee and Maggie Valley. Follow the signs to Cherokee and you will backtrack across a less-traveled section of Route 19 through the entire width of the reservation. Things get a bit congested at the 19/441 junction, but it's nothing like the standstill stuff you'd have experienced if you had taken 441 out of the park and into Cherokee.

If you'd rather forgo the entire reservation, stay on the Blue Ridge for one more exit (roughly twelve more miles) and get off at Waynesville/Sylva. Both papermill towns have quaint downtowns in various stages of restoration and there are plenty of interesting shops and restaurants.

Sorry, if you're headed west toward Bryson City, there's no way to avoid town altogether. You *can* save a bit of aggravation coming from the park by taking the next left after the Blue Ridge Parkway entrance at the big brown park service sign that says "To Big Cove Road commercial campgrounds." That little stretch of road is Saunoke Bridge Road. Take a right onto Big Cove Road, a left at the stoplight, followed by a quick right onto Acquoni Road. This puts you on the less-traveled, locals-side of the Oconaluftee River. Instead of tacky tourist shops and red lights, you'll pass Cherokee High School and reservation social service offices. The views aren't anything, but at least you're not sucking exhaust fumes and you're moving. The one stoplight is at the end of the road where it merges with Route 19. Take a left toward Maggie Valley or a right toward Bryson City.

Secret Information

For more information about Cherokee, North Carolina, call the chamber of commerce at (704) 497-9195.

TOP SECRET

If you want to find true traditional Native American souvenirs in Cherokee, you have to hunt a bit. There are a few places that specialize in genuine items made in town by the Cherokee, the trademark name of the reservation-owned company that produces drums, moccasins, clothing, and other Native American souvenirs. Make sure any items you buy have the Cherokee's manila-colored tag, which on the back reads "Made in America by Native Americans."

Locator Map

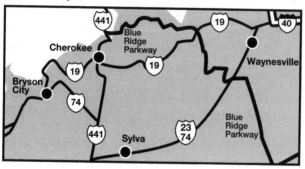

79

Night Moves

Every afternoon at about four or five, people start pouring out of the Great Smoky Mountains National Park. Pity. The action's just beginning and there's a lot to do in the park as it gets dark. Park rangers lead a variety of programs as the sun sets; most are attended by those camping overnight, but the programs are completely open to anyone who wants to attend, whether they're spending the night in the park or not.

At Cades Cove, for example, rangers lead sunset hikes six days a week from early June through late August. The moderately challenging, one-hour, one-mile walks lead to an overlook above the cove where trekkers can watch the sun go down. Later, beginning at nine, nightly presentations and slide shows cover such topics as the history of the cove and the diversity of biosystems within the Smokies. On the south side of the park, the Oconaluftee Visitors Center is the site of late evening programs that explore the native plants of the area and focus on fireflies. Nearby, the Mountain Farm Museum is the venue for expert and hilarious storytelling on Friday nights from late June until early August. At the Deep Creek picnic area further southwest, parents and kids get together to search for bugs and reptiles during the early evening family program. And starting at eight or later at Smokemont, which is at the southern end of Newfound Gap Road, there are ninety-minute hikes, during which rangers talk about the wildlife that lurks somewhere in the ever-deepening shadows of the forest and offer slide shows that tell about the history of the Cherokee.

These fascinating and free events are more than enough reason to hang around the park as night falls. Even if you don't participate in a formal program, it's nice to drive its roads or take a short hike as dusk settles. The early evening hours are a prime time to spot wildlife emerging to forage for food and there's a peacefulness that can't be duplicated during the heat of the day. On a clear night, the park, which is away from most of the light pollution of civilization, is a prime spot to park and watch the stars put on a spectacular show in the sky.

Secret Information

For information and a schedule of nighttime programs in the park, pick up the *Smokies Guide*, the park's newspaper, available for a twenty-five-cent donation at the visitors centers and other places in the park.

TOP SECRET

Nowhere in the world but Southeast Asia and the Great Smoky Mountains National Park's Elkmont area can you see synchronized fireflies—groups of insects whose tails all glow at the same time in an entertaining light show. The strange phenomenon—likely a form of communication—takes place around Elkmont, which is off Little River Road on the Tennessee side of the park, during the three weeks in June that the bugs breed. Ask a park ranger about the best time and place to see the fireflies for yourself.

80

Farm Family

As you walk the grounds of the Yellow Branch Farm, remind yourself that you are in North Carolina, not Switzerland. The brown cheese-making building, perched on the side of the hill, hints of the Alps. Wildflowers fill the front yard of the farmhouse. A couple of cows graze on a grassy slope. A berry garden, fruit trees, and a vegetable garden are busy producing food for the residents of this fifty-acre farm, through which the Yellow Branch stream flows. Go on, take a deep breath and start yodeling.

This genuine working farm just happens to offer a couple of treats for visitors driving near the Fontana Village area (Secret 12), south of the Great Smoky Mountains National Park. It's owned by Dudley and Sally DeGroot and tended year-round by their son, Bruce, and his wife, Karen Mickler. The four not only grow food but also pursue personal passions on the land: Bruce is also a carpenter; Sally operates a nursery specializing in wild North Carolina azaleas; and Karen is an accomplished potter, who sells her work from a no-frills pottery shop in a frame house with a nice front porch.

Collectors of handmade pottery will adore browsing the array of stoneware, ovenware, tableware, and decorative ware, such as vases, lamps, and candleholders, in the tiny front room of Mickler's store. In back is her workshop, decorated only with work tools and pottery-making equipment and splatters of clay that she molds and fires into functional works of art. Although Mickler hates to talk about herself, it's clear that being an artisan is not merely her livelihood but also her life. She uses only lead-free, nontoxic glazes, and every piece is handmade, not cast, so no two are exactly alike. The standard price for a four-piece place setting is seventy dollars, although less expensive small vases and spoon rests sell well because they make nice gifts. Mickler, a professional artisan of more than twenty years' experience, keeps casual hours at the shop. She does chores in the

Yellow Branch Farm is a genuine working farm as well as a unique destination for tourists.

morning and operates her business in the afternoon, but she says you can catch her "by chance or appointment."

The other main attraction at Yellow Branch is homemade cheese created about twice a week in a tiny one-room building full of stainless steel equipment and coolers. The idea for this venture was whetted when one of the DeGroots' two cows—Meadow Beauty and Tiger Lily, who graze on pesticide- and herbicide-free pastureland—started yielding four gallons of milk a day. Mickler immediately set out to learn the cheese-making process from a book, then she enrolled in a course at the University of Wisconsin. In 1985 the farm was licensed to make and sell cheese. Mickler came up with original recipes for both plain—kind of a cross between Muenster and Monterey Jack—and peppered cheese, the latter of which recently won a national cheese-making award and is flavored with jalapeño.

The odd combination of a working family farm, a tiny cheese-making operation, and a pottery shop out in the middle of nowhere gives Yellow Branch a casual charm. To Mickler it's not so strange, it's just the simple way that she and her family have chosen to live. "Farming is a way of life, not a livelihood," she says. "We are sort of homesteading."

Secret Information

Location: Off North Carolina Highway 28, heading from Fontana Village to Bryson City, North Carolina. The signs do not mention Yellow Branch Farm; just look for those marked "Pottery" and "Cheese."

Address: Route 2, Box 176E, Yellow Branch Road, Robbinsville, North Carolina 28771.

Phone: (704) 479-6710 (evenings).

Hours: By appointment or drop in during the afternoon to have the best chance of catching someone in the pottery or cheese shop.

Credit cards: MasterCard, Visa.

TOP SECRET

Karen Mickler, one of the owners of Yellow Branch Farm Cheese and Pottery, enjoys seeing her younger visitors get their hands in the clay she uses in her pottery shop. If you are traveling with children, mention this to her, and she will soon have those little hands squishing and squashing clay creations.

"In" Place in the Mountains

81

A sign in the lobby of the Mountain Harbor Inn reads, "I wasn't born in the South, but I got here as fast as I could." That sums up the sentiment of innkeepers Jim and Shirley McEwan, who moved from Ann Arbor, Michigan, to open up a flowery southern inn just off I-40 on the shore of Douglas Lake in Tennessee. The pair had retired and were looking for something to do, when their friends and now business partners, Rich and Pat Steinaway, stumbled upon this former fishing camp and bait shop. The two couples renovated it into a three-story, white-sided and green-shuttered twelve-room hideaway overlooking the lake.

The McEwans have created an atmosphere of southern country charm. The color scheme has a feminine feel—lots of greens, pinks, and lavender. Flowers are everywhere—in baskets hanging from the inn's windows on the highway side; in window boxes full of geraniums and periwinkles on the water side; in several flower beds blooming with irises in the spring and perennials such as daylilies, scarlet sage, and daisies in the summer. Inside, flowery touches are everywhere, but be forewarned—if you don't appreciate artificial lavender and green wisteria vines and other faux floral arrangements you might find Mountain Inn's tea-party feel isn't your cup of tea.

The decor of each room centers around a quilt and a different theme. The red and green quilt in the Fisherman's Room, for instance, complements furniture made out of sturdy tree branches and fish mounted on the walls. The First Lady's Suite, which got its name when Don Sundquist and his wife, Martha, stayed in the room during his successful campaign for governor of Tennessee, is adorned in bright green, bright blue, and pink. For a dose of patriotic decor, choose the Americana room, which is appropriately done in red, white, and blue.

The inn draws guests from all over the world, including many from Great Britain. It's a popular place for family reunions and weddings—

Mountain Harbor Inn is a hideaway, yes, as well as a haven for weddings and family reunions.

the wrought-iron arched arbor on the lawn next to the lake is the site of approximately forty or so "I dos" a year. The big draw is the view of the thirty-five-hundred-square-mile lake and, on most days, the Great Smoky Mountains beyond. Guests like to sit out on the porches of their rooms—all of which face the lake—and watch the sky change as evening thunderstorms roll in over the water.

Those who seek more excitement are only a few miles from Pigeon Forge, Gatlinburg, and the Great Smoky Mountains National Park. Dandridge is just to the west and Cowboys on the Water (Secret 42) is only a couple miles east. There are several golf courses within ten miles or so and the McEwans will help arrange boating or fishing excursions on the lake.

Breakfast, which is included in the room price, is served in the inn's restaurant, which is open to the public for lunch and dinner every day except Wednesday. Entrees such as filet mignon and prime rib range in price from $12.95 to $19.95. The recently closed-in porch area means that diners can now savor the view but don't have to run for cover if a sudden storm hits.

Secret Information

Location: On Tennessee Highway 139, east of Dandridge, Tennessee.
Address: 1199 Highway 139, Dandridge, Tennessee 37725.
Phone: (423) 397-3345 or (423) 397-0264.
Web site: www.smoky.mtnmall.com/mall/mtharbor.html.
E-mail: mtharbor@smokymtnmall.com.
Season: Year-round; office and restaurant closed on Wednesday.
Rates: $85 to $125 a night.
Credit cards: American Express, Discover, MasterCard, Visa.

TOP SECRET

A delightful Victorian high tea is served at the Mountain Harbor Inn each Saturday afternoon from 2:00 P.M. until 5:00 P.M. The price is $12.95 for an array of delicacies such as quiche, scones with Devonshire cream, cucumber sandwiches, and, of course, tea and other beverages. Reservations are required.

82

Going Downhill

The Great Smoky Mountains aren't known as great skiing mountains. When downhillers want to hit the slopes, they usually opt to head west to the Rockies or north to New England for deep powder and challenging runs. That's just fine with the local folks in western North Carolina and East Tennessee, because then they have more room to schuss and snowboard at one of the Smokies' best-kept winter secrets—Cataloochee Ski Area.

Cataloochee, situated in Maggie Valley, North Carolina, is no Aspen or Vail or even Waterville Valley. What it is, however, is a well-run, friendly, family-owned and operated ski area with nine trails and a mile-high location (fifty-four hundred feet at the highest peak), which is ideal for making and keeping snow. So even if the mercury is nearing fifty degrees in downtown Maggie Valley or Gatlinburg (or on the slopes at its lower-elevation Tennessee counterpart, Ober Gatlinburg), there's plenty of snow up on Cataloochee to keep beginners, intermediates, and even some die-hard black diamond experts happy.

Since 1940 descendants of the Alexander family, who also own and operate nearby Cataloochee Ranch (Secret 25), have been sharing their mountain with skiers. The ski area borders the Great Smoky Mountains National Park and was named after Cataloochee Valley. It is North Carolina's oldest ski area and the best choice for Smokies visitors who either ski or would like to try the sport for the first time.

Cataloochee's special twenty-five-dollar Learn to Ski package, offered every nonholiday, Monday through Thursday, from January 5 until the end of the season, is an inexpensive way for first-time skiers ages eight and older to test the slopes. The fee includes a beginner lesson, beginner's lift ticket, and rental skis, poles, and boots. For kids four through twelve there are half-day and full-day ski school classes taught by professionally trained instructors. These lessons range from thirty-five to sixty-five dollars, depending on age and class length. The

A sunny day of freshly fallen powder makes Cataloochee a skier's paradise. (Photo courtesy of Cataloochee Ski Area)

ski school even offers snowboard instruction for both kids and adults. Snowboard rentals are available for twenty-five dollars per session.

Although Cataloochee's spacious and gentle bottom mountain terrain is ideal for beginners, the two mountaintop expert runs and four intermediate trails offer not only challenging skiing but also panoramic views of the surrounding snow-covered Smokies. The winter wonderland scenery is so breathtaking on the intermediate High Meadow run, which hugs the outer boundaries of the ski area, that you might forget to keep your eyes on the trail. But, as with every southern ski area, at Cataloochee you must stay alert for other skiers in your path. During the Christmas season in particular, the majority of Cataloochee's skiers (and we'll use that term loosely) are first-timers or novices up from Florida to see some snow. A few of them stacked together in a fallen pile of skis and poles can turn a beginner slope into an expert obstacle course real fast.

If you can swing it, midweek at Cataloochee is the best time to ski. The slopes aren't congested with weekend youth groups and tourists, and the local North Carolinians are an open-arms bunch. You'll also enjoy reduced weekday rates (twenty dollars full day/ fifteen dollars half day for adults versus thirty-three and twenty-six dollars, respectively, on weekends). A midweek stay also means more leg room for stretching out in front of the circular fireplace in Cataloochee's rustic ski lodge or soaking up the sun on the slopeside outdoor deck. On both weekdays and weekends, lift tickets are free for children six and under and adults aged sixty-five and up.

Secret Information

Location: Maggie Valley, North Carolina.

Address: 1080 Ski Lodge Road, Maggie Valley, North Carolina 28751.

Phone: (800) 768-0285 or (704) 926-0285.

Web site: www.cataloochee.com.

Prices: Weekday: adults $20, students $16, juniors (7–12) $13; Saturday/ holiday: adults $33, students $33, juniors $23; Sunday: adults $31, students $31, juniors $21.

Details: Cataloochee features two double chairlifts and one rope tow. The top elevation is 5,400 feet and the steepest vertical drop is 740 feet. There are nine groomed slopes and trails; all but two are equipped with snow-making machinery. The Cataloochee Ski Lodge includes a restaurant, ski and rental shops, rest rooms, and common areas.

TOP SECRET

There's nothing quite like gliding down a snowy Smoky Mountains slope under a blanket of twinkling stars. You can give it a try at Cataloochee Ski Area simply by waiting for the parking lot to clear out at suppertime and bundling up for some brisk night skiing. From 6:00 P.M. until 10:00 P.M. every Tuesday through Saturday from December 19 through February 28, and on selected holiday Sundays and Mondays, the lights go up on the slopes and the skiers, the sun, and the lift ticket prices go down. It's only fifteen dollars weekday and eighteen dollars weekend for adults to ski at night. There's also a twilight ticket available on the same days, which allows you to ski from 1:00 P.M. until 10:00 P.M. The extra five hours only bump up the lift ticket five dollars during the week, but it will cost you an extra fifteen dollars on the weekends.

Smokies Stories

83

This entry might seem out of place in a travel book that aims to pry people away from the living room sofa and into the great outdoors to explore back roads and hidden spots. But if you'd like to learn more about the heritage of southern Appalachia, sit back down in front of the TV set for a few moments and tune into *The Heartland Series*.

The program first aired in 1984 to celebrate the fiftieth anniversary of the Great Smoky Mountains National Park. Since then, host Bill Landry and a crack team of producers and videographers have collected stories about the people, history, and culture of East Tennessee. Landry has become the local version of the late Charles Kuralt—someone gifted with the folksy ability to sit down with and draw stories out of everyone from beekeepers to square dancers.

The Heartland Series is produced by and airs on WBIR-TV in Knoxville, Tennessee, Monday through Friday at 6:25 A.M., 11:30 P.M., and 12:30 P.M. Installments are just under four minutes long, but they are carefully crafted stories. More than eight hundred segments are in the can, with titles such as "A. D.'s Bear Stories," "Wiley Oakley's 'The Cow Barn,' " "Confessions of a Moonshiner," and "Berry Picking." *Heartland* episodes sometimes touch people in unexpected ways. Landry recounts the time the station received a call at three in the morning after a man in Chicago saw an episode featuring the Knoxville Giants, an all-black baseball team on which his grandfather had played. He saw his granddad's picture on the episode and immediately called the station to see if he could order the tape.

Yep. You can buy tapes. Seventeen volumes of the series are now on video, each with one and three-quarters to two hours of material. Repackaged stories also have run on the Travel Channel under the title *Appalachian Stories: The Heartland Series*. The program is available in American embassies all over the world to educate foreigners about Appalachian culture.

Landry attributes much of the show's success to the fact that it "tries to allow the people of the region to tell their own stories. The stories we tell are tied to the land, the seasons, and the cycles of life, like picking and breaking beans on the front porch in summertime or sleigh riding at Christmas." Landry's personal favorite? "The one I'm working on right now had better be my favorite."

Secret Information

A free catalog of *Heartland Series* videotapes is available by writing WBIR-TV, *The Heartland Series*, 1513 Hutchinson Avenue, Knoxville, Tennessee 37917. Tapes are also on sale in visitors centers and gift shops throughout the area.

Prices: Volumes 1–17 are $29.95 each; specials are $14.95 each; order six or more tapes from WBIR-TV and $29.95 tapes are discounted to $25.

Credit cards: Call (423) 637-1010 to order with a MasterCard or Visa.

TOP SECRET

The seventeen volumes of *The Heartland Series* available on video are collections of up to thirty-five segments, each almost four minutes long, capturing small slices of Appalachian culture. Also available are four specials, each priced at $14.95, that take a more in-depth look at their subjects. Our favorite is the twenty-five-minute "Cades Cove: The Home Place," in which series host Bill Landry and his production team lovingly tell the story of one of the Smokies' earliest communities, which vanished when residents were forced to move away to make way for the national park.

Ramsay Cascades

Tall Falls

84

You know those feats in life you perform and think you're going to die while you're in the middle of them, but after you're finished, you're tremendously glad you persevered? Such acts of courage, determination, and accomplishment can never be taken away from you. Hiking to Ramsay Cascades in the northeast part of the Great Smoky Mountains National Park is one such feat. The secret here is that while the Great Smoky Mountains National Park considers the trek "strenuous," it's doable for those who aren't hard-core hikers. Folks who are only moderately fit might feel winded as they get into the fourth mile of this eight-mile, round-trip hike, but the reward at the end of the climb up makes the effort well worth it.

The trail, which starts near Greenbrier Cove on the Tennessee side of the park, is deceiving for the first mile and a half because hikers walk along a roadbed next to a tributary of the Little Pigeon River. When the path crosses a bridge, the trail suddenly becomes steeper and more difficult. Leafy tunnels through the trees lead through this virgin forest and open onto picturesque scenes of small waterfalls in the stream. There are a multitude of ferns and moss-covered rocks. Large, raised tree roots make the trail hazardous in some places. These roots often hug rocks and intertwine with other tree roots. Some of the poplars along the way are huge, so fat that five people with arms outstretched can hardly reach around them.

As the climb continues, sometimes aided by flat rocks that have been placed as steps in particularly steep sections, other sights, such as the massive rhododendrons, become dominant. The view from the trail takes on a jungle appearance, and, at times, the trail seems to end abruptly because overgrowth hides it. Be careful, because the trail drops off dramatically in several places on the side next to the stream.

The junglelike tree canopy allows in very little sunlight, but in places where the sun sneaks through, light reflects off intricate spider

The view of the falls at Ramsay Cascades makes the hard hike worth the time and effort. (Photo courtesy of Great Smoky Mountains National Park)

webs. As the trail finishes the fourth mile, hikers have to jump rocks across a stream and do a small amount of rock climbing.

The payoff for all this effort is the first glimpse of Ramsay Cascades, a wall of rock over which water tumbles down approximately one hundred feet. The mist from the cascades sprays travelers while they rest on a boulder at the bottom and savor their accomplishment. In the afterglow of meeting the challenge of getting to the cascades, the four-mile walk back down the trail doesn't seem nearly so tough.

Secret Information

Location: The trail to Ramsay Cascades starts off a road from the Greenbrier entrance to the national park, which is on U.S. Highway 321 between Gatlinburg and Cosby, Tennessee.

Details: Set aside five hours (two and a half hours up, a half-hour at the cascades, and two hours down) for the hike.

TOP SECRET

If you're looking for a somewhat less-strenuous hike to a waterfall than the hike to Ramsay Cascades, check out the little-known Meigs Creek Trail to Meigs Creek Falls. A simple sign reading "Trail" marks the trailhead at the back of the Sinks area parking lot on Little River Road about three miles east of the Townsend, Tennessee, entrance to the Great Smoky Mountains National Park. It's four miles uphill to the falls, and although they are only about twenty-five-feet high, they're clear, cool, and raging. Venture on to discover another secret cascade just up the trail.

85

Down by the
Old Mill Stream

Across a one-lane bridge off U.S. Highway 321 in the Smokies foothills lies a red-brick, two-story home overlooking a small dam and waterfall, the former site of the nineteenth-century Little River Mill. Around the turn of the century it did a thriving business grinding cornmeal and snowbird flour. Owner William Peery built the home for his family in 1929. His sons took over the mill in the fifties and ran it until it closed in the early seventies.

Today the unassuming-looking dwelling is the Mill House Restaurant, a haven of fine dining and Continental comfort tucked in the Walland Gap of Chilhowee Mountain in Tennessee. Maine native Richard Estes and his wife, Diana, took it over in the early eighties. At first, the couple tried to supplement their food-service income by devoting the upstairs to a gallery featuring art and antiques from Europe. Unfortunately, fine imports didn't offer much appeal to the local truck and trailer crowd, so the couple converted the space to a residence for themselves and their four children.

The restaurant's interior, however, retains a casual European feel. To enter, customers ring a bell, then open the front door, causing the other patrons to look up in unison with each new arrival. Dining areas are decorated in rose, forest green, and burgundy. A print of *The Blue Boy* hangs on the living room wall near a fireplace that blazes in chilly weather. Touches that remind you you're still in Tennessee, however, include a dulcimer resting on the mantel.

The food combines European and country flavor. The menu is *table d'hôte* or *prix fixe*, a fancy French way of saying that all dinners are the same price ($18.95, plus gratuities and taxes) and include everything you would want—appetizers; soups; salads; main courses like steak, catfish, shrimp, pork, tuna, or chicken; vegetables; and desserts. The signature entree is steak Diana, named for the owner. Another customer favorite is chicken galantine, a boneless

The dining experience at the Mill House Restaurant combines European flair with country flavor.

breast served with seafood mousse. Diana makes all the desserts like orange cream cake, key lime pie, and Little River mud pie.

The pace is leisurely, and the Esteses encourage customers to linger and enjoy their meals. Plan on at least an hour and a half, although Richard recommends staying two and a half. The secluded spot is a favorite of locals looking for privacy, including Japanese executives, who chose the place to seal a deal to build a new Nippon automobile parts plant in Tennessee. Diners who came through the doors as strangers have even been known to strike up friendships between courses.

Secret Information

Location: Just across the Little River from U.S. Highway 321, north of Townsend.

Address: 4537 Old Walland Highway, Walland, Tennessee 37886.

Phone: (423) 982-5726.

Fax: (423) 681-1040.

Hours: 5:00 P.M. to 10:00 P.M., Friday and Saturday.

Season: Year-round.

Prices: All meals are $18.95 (plus gratuities and taxes) and include seven courses.

Credit cards: American Express, MasterCard, Visa.

Reservations: Not necessary but recommended.

Details: Casual clothing is fine. Bring your own liquor and the staff will serve it for $1 a person.

TOP SECRET

The homey front porch of the Mill House Restaurant overlooking the old gristmill dam and waterfall is a favorite place for diners to sit before or after a meal. Just ask Richard Estes or another member of the staff and you can have appetizers or dessert served there.

⌂ Hickory Haven

Tree House

86

When innkeepers Connie Nicholson and her partner John Eukers first opened Hickory Haven, they feared that no one would ever find their secluded North Carolina inn. We can understand why. The road leading to Hickory Haven is a winding gravel cowpath wide enough for only one vehicle. The inn is set so deep back in the woods that visitors might think they're lost. As the route winds through the towering trees, suddenly the inn appears on the left like a mirage—two elegant Victorian homes blended together as one.

"We're hidden so completely in the trees that when we started we were worried about getting people to come out here," says Nicholson, a portrait artist, whose mother, Shirley Crakes, bought Hickory Haven for her daughter to run. "It turns out this is exactly what our guests want—peace and quiet. People see our web page and say, 'Yes, this is what I'm looking for—a place to relax away from it all.' "

Situated at midtree level, the inn has the feel of a grown-up's treehouse. The trees envelop it, making it seem like a natural part of the surrounding woods. The building's interior feels cozy, which is remarkable considering its large size. The multiple common areas, decorated with antiques and collectibles, have plenty of comfy chairs and couches and fireplaces plus unique built-ins like the spiral staircase leading up from the kitchen to the most popular guest rooms—the Romeo and the Juliet.

The right half of the inn was built in 1912 and is a tad more worn but just as welcoming as the house-sized addition on the left, constructed in 1988. Guest rooms are situated on both sides and range from simply charming bedrooms to spacious suites complete with a private balcony and separate sitting room with fireplace. Many rooms have a whirlpool bath and all include the bountiful "everything but the kitchen sink" brunch that Connie concocts daily.

Hickory Haven's porch at midtree level gives visitors a sense of being in a tree house.

"Between the food and the conversation, it's really more of an event than a meal," she says.

The new section, with its turrets, wraparound decks, and gleaming hardwood floors, was built by the previous owner, who, Nicholson learned, was a "rather eccentric" Key West, Florida, bank-president-turned-Budweiser-distributor. "If you look closely at the railing you'll see the double-headed eagle in the design," Nicholson says. "We knew that was a Bavarian thing, but for the longest time we didn't realize that we had the Anheuser Busch symbol out there on the porch."

Secret Information

Location: Off U.S. Highway 23/74 in Balsam, south of Waynesville, North Carolina.

Address: P.O. Box 88, Balsam, North Carolina 28707.

Phone: (800) 684-2836 or (704) 452-1106.

Fax: (704) 456-4830.

E-mail: smkymtbb@primeline.com.

Web site: www.primeline.com/~smkymtbb.

Season: Open year-round, except January.

Rates: $85 to $130.

Credit cards: MasterCard, Visa.

TOP SECRET

Hickory Haven is surrounded by a web of hiking trails that lead around the property and into the nearby mountains. Before you strike off, wait for large and lovable Bernie, the inn's resident Collie-Saint Bernard mix. "Nobody taught her this, but when Bernie sees what path you're going to take, she gets in front of you and shows you where to go," Nicholson says. "I don't know why she does it, except that she loves our guests. She's the first one to greet everyone as they come in. She's our diplomat."

87

Little Vine of Horrors

Remember *Little Shop of Horrors*, the Broadway musical and movie? It was about a humongous plant that liked to devour people. Well, the Smokies have their own version of a voracious piece of greenery—a semiwoody vine with hairy stems imported from the Far East that swallows up telephone poles, road signs, water towers, abandoned cars, even entire buildings, but, we're thankful, not human beings.

This frightening foliage is called kudzu, a name that even sounds like a B-movie monster (Now playing: *Godzilla Meets Kudzu*). A member of the pea family with relatives that include soybeans and black-eyed peas, it's a trailing or climbing vine that boasts six-inch-long leaves, reddish-purple flowers that grow in twelve-inch-long spikelike clusters and smell like grape Kool-Aid, and four-inch-long hairy fruit. Under the right conditions, it can grow up to a foot a day; it can climb up to sixty feet above the ground and its roots can dig twelve feet deep. Once it stakes out a certain spot, it's nearly impossible to kill. As you drive through the Smoky Mountains area, you can see it covering entire roadsides in a mass of huge leaves.

This blight, it turns out, was intentionally inflicted on the mountains. Kudzu was originally introduced to this country during the 1876 Centennial Exposition in Philadelphia. At first it was embraced as a great way to shade porches, feed livestock, and conserve soil. In the thirties and early forties millions of kudzu plants were sown throughout the South, and by 1945 it covered half a million acres. That's about when folks began to notice that kudzu was a little too good at growing and that, like a mutant plant straight out of a Stephen King novel, it tended to strangle trees to death. Sometime in the early 1970s, it was officially declared a weed, but the nuisance designation came too late. Today kudzu covers seven million acres and that's expected to double by early in the next century. Fortunately, the Great Smoky Mountains National Park has embarked

Kudzu has been creeping around in America since it was brought here for the 1876 Centennial Exposition in Philadelphia. (Photo courtesy of Diane Hoots)

on an eradication program that has gotten rid of most of the vile vine within its boundaries, although spots from which kudzu has been cleared need to be checked for five years to make sure it doesn't come back.

Then there are the people who see kudzu not as a threat to envelop the planet but as a productive cash crop. It's reportedly good for treating alcoholism, can be used in cooking, and might be used to make textiles or paper. Monstrous or misunderstood, you decide, but be forewarned when you visit the Smokies: Don't sit still too long or you might fall prey to the *Attack of the Killer Kudzu.*

Secret Information

To learn more about kudzu, check out the Amazing World of Kudzu World Wide Web site at www.sa.ua.edu/cptr/kudzu.htm or, for a fun fictional look at the horrors of kudzu, pick up *Kudzu Crypt: Dark Visions to Haunt and Entwine You* (Earthtide Publications), a collection of scary short stories edited by Beryl Lumpkin and available at the Earthtide Gallery (Secret 5).

Who knew that kudzu was so useful? Diane Hoots, the owner of Krazy Kudzu Products of Warner Robins, Georgia, has made a business out of selling stuff made from the vile vine. She travels to exhibitions in the South to hawk kudzu jelly, kudzu candy, kudzu baskets, kudzu candles, kudzu wall hangings, T-shirts that read "The Vine That Ate the South," and more. She calls herself the Kudzu Guru and got into the kudzu business in 1993 because, she says, "No one else was doing it." (We can't imagine why.) She's even written (with Juanita Baldwin) a tribute to the prolific plant, called *Kudzu: The Vine to Love or Hate* (Suntop Press) that tells its history and details its many uses. To order the book or a catalog of kudzu products, contact Hoots at P.O. Box 8584, Warner Robins, Georgia 31095-8584, or call (912) 922-6300.

On-Road Adventure

88

So, are you up for a little wilderness adventure without leaving the comfort of your car? Check out the loop through the southeastern part of the Great Smoky Mountains National Park called Heintooga-Round Bottom Road. Starting at the Blue Ridge Parkway just north of Soco Gap in North Carolina, the route takes you high into the mountains to a spot called Round Bottom. It then twists and turns back to lower elevations through the Indian reservation and, finally, into Cherokee. The climb up offers panoramic views of mountains. The trip down ranks right up there with anything a ride at Disney World or Six Flags has to offer.

Start the drive by heading north on Heintooga Ridge Road off the Blue Ridge Parkway—the first stretch is a spur of the parkway, in fact. The paved two-way road passes into the national park and ends at the 5,535-foot-high Heintooga Overlook near the Balsam Mountain Campground (Secret 37). There a sign says, "Heintooga-Round Bottom Road." This might be a bit confusing because we haven't been able to find a road with that name on any map. Indeed, the park service's trail map labels it as Balsam Mountain Road. The well-maintained gravel road is a little bumpy but perfectly passable in a car or van (expect to invest in a car wash afterward).

What lies ahead on this serpentine and sometimes muddy mountain road is a canopy of trees above and a carpet of leaves and vegetation below. For many of us, the road that climbs the crest of Balsam Mountain is the closest we'll ever get to driving through a rain forest. The sun peeks through at breaks in the leaves, but mainly it's a cool, almost cavernous drive. There is no shoulder, unless you count the steep drop on the left to the valley floor below. Chances are good that you'll travel the entire secluded stretch without seeing another vehicle or person.

At Round Bottom, a flat open area that offers a good spot to stop and savor the mountain air, the route becomes Straight Fork Road.

At one point your path appears to be blocked by a river. Relax. The road leads through the river (quite shallow at this point), as some Cherokee trout fisherman pointed out to us as they waved our van across the rippling water.

The park ends at the boundary of the Cherokee Indian Reservation and the community of Big Cove. Follow Straight Fork Road until it intersects with Big Cove Road, then hang a left. Big Cove will lead you into the heart of the Cherokee hubbub, a stark contrast to the wonderful wilderness you've just left behind.

Secret Information

Location: Off the Blue Ridge Parkway, on the southeastern border of the Great Smoky Mountains National Park in North Carolina.

For information about conditions, call the Oconaluftee Visitors Center at (704) 497-9146 or the park headquarters at (423) 436-1200.

TOP SECRET

As you leave Heintooga-Round Bottom Road behind and travel along the Straight Fork and Big Cove Roads toward Cherokee, you'll notice Native American fishermen casting for trout. The Qualla Boundary reservation features thirty miles of fast-flowing trout streams and three ponds stocked twice weekly with rainbow, brown, and brook trout. All you need to drop a line of your own is a five-dollar daily reservation fishing permit (available at several stores in Cherokee). No state license is required, and there's a ten-fish limit. Call Fish and Game Management Enterprise at (800) 438-1601 or (704) 497-5201 for more information on fishing on the reservation.

89

The Well House

Well-Hidden Treasure

Most of the tourists visiting Dillsboro, a postcard-perfect mountain village in North Carolina, never cross over the railroad tracks that run through downtown. There's plenty to do in the city center, and climbing the hill on the other side of the tracks might not seem worth the effort on a steamy summer afternoon. Then again, the Well House sits on top of that little hill, and it is worth it.

The Well House is situated in the eclectic jumble of wood and stone known as the Rivershops. This site is where the town's first residents—Mr. and Mrs. William Allen Dill—built their home. In fact, the restaurant was built around the family's well, hand dug during the early 1880s to supply water for the Dills. It is still used occasionally to irrigate the plants. The riggings, bricks, and bucket are the originals.

The well is a funky feature of the restaurant, but it's the food, friendly atmosphere, and cool (as in temperature) surroundings that draw well-dressed women and guys with office jobs up the steep, daylily-covered slope from downtown Dillsboro. Stepping down into the restaurant (it sits a couple of feet below street level) is like coming upon an underground cavern. The low windows and wooden booths help keep the place dark and comfortable even on the worst scorcher. Big band-era music plays on the rickety sound system, and cutout ads and articles from old *Life* magazines adorn the walls. Locals swap friendly greetings and munch on hot deli sandwiches and specialties like chicken cashew salad (with apple chunks) on freshly baked bread and Cuban pork chops with saffron rice. On cooler days a round wooden table on the outside front terrace offers a pleasant, shady spot for lunch.

At the Well House, you don't even have to throw a coin in the well to get your wish for a wonderful place to eat.

The Well House looks relatively inconspicuous from the outside, but the interior resembles an underground tavern as you step down through the restaurant door.

Secret Information

Location: Downtown Dillsboro, North Carolina.

Address: P.O. Box 580, Dillsboro, North Carolina 28725.

Phone: (704) 586-8588.

Hours: 11:00 A.M. to 7:00 P.M.; sometimes the restaurant is open later during the summer.

Prices: Lunch $2.65 to $4.25; dinner $6.95 to $10.95.

Credit cards: None.

TOP SECRET

If you're taking a trip on the Great Smoky Mountains Railway (Secret 29), call up the Well House and order a picnic box lunch to take along. They'll pack you a hearty sandwich, drink, and dessert and have it ready for pickup before your departure.

Great Smoky Arts and Crafts Community

Craftsmen at Work

90

As you're driving through the Smokies, take a moment to imagine what it must have been like to live here 150 years ago—no paved roads, no electricity, no phones, no plumbing, no Wal-Marts, no McDonald's, nothing but rugged wilderness, snowbound winters, and a life dedicated to providing the basics for a family.

This is the world the mountain people of Appalachia inhabited not so long ago. To make life livable they used their fertile imaginations and considerable survival skills to design and create tools, clothing, shelter, furnishings, and other objects by hand and from scratch. It is this world that the Great Smoky Arts and Crafts Community is dedicated to preserving. Modern life has come to the mountains, but members of the group continue to practice the crafts of the early settlers. What was first created for survival has now become art.

As early as 1937 a few hardy artists began what was then known as the Glades Crafts Tour. Their mission was to maintain a sense of history and to honor the resourcefulness of their forefathers (and mothers). Over the years a few of the craftsmen, some of whom had lived in the area for years, would go into downtown Gatlinburg and set up a table or booth along the street and demonstrate their skills. They sometimes sold items to passersby, who then wanted to visit their shops and learn more about the artists' work. From this casual beginning was created the artist colony centered around Glades and Buckhorn Roads off U.S. Highway 321, just north of downtown Gatlinburg, Tennessee. It wasn't until 1976, however, that a group of twenty-three craftsmen banded together to formally create a nonprofit organization. A couple years later they started to call themselves the Great Smoky Arts and Crafts Community. Among the current seventy-one businesses in the organization are ones run by second- and third-generation owners, and their products are true to the originals.

Shopaholics will have a ball driving the eight-mile loop of shops, studios, and galleries hunting for wood carvings and hand-woven

The Great Smoky Arts and Crafts Community is filled with funky shops where you can buy everything from handmade brooms to teddy bears that have been baked in an oven.

tapestries, blown glass and baskets, stained glass and leather goods, pewter and pottery, watercolors and photography, candles and clothing. Small stone or log shops—some also the artists' homes—are scattered everywhere along the roads, on hilltops and in quiet coves. Many are working studios, like Gatlinburg Ceramics, which is owned by Judy Bailey, a nationally certified ceramist. She enjoys describing her art to visitors and points out, "We have over five thousand molds in the shop, and we created each one of them. Every piece is made here, from first casting to final hand glazing and painting. Each piece is an original."

Part of the fun of poking through different shops is seeing the contrast between what different creators think of as art. The folks at Ogle's Broom Shop, one of the colony's original eight businesses, sells authentic Appalachian handmade brooms, while Earthspeak specializes in pen-and-ink drawings of Native American themes and has a distinctly New Age feel. Some places, like Karen's Kreations, cater to collectors and hawk handmade dolls that can cost more than six hundred dollars. Others have rather odd niches: Baked Bears, for example, makes traditional teddy bears, then bakes them in a kiln to give their fur an antique feel. Then there are the I-don't-know-much-about-art-but-I-know-what-sells shops like Adoughable Things-Shucks Y'all, which hawks knickknacks made from hardened dough and corn shucks.

The Great Smoky Arts and Crafts Community recently celebrated its sixtieth year. Who knows, maybe in another sixty years there will be a new generation of artists dedicated to preserving the traditions of today—antique cellular phones, authentic Nikes, handmade Big Macs? Nah.

Secret Information

Location: The Great Smoky Arts and Crafts Community loop is off U.S. Highway 321, east of Gatlinburg, Tennessee.

Details: A brochure with detailed map of the Arts and Crafts Community loop is available in Gatlinburg at many businesses and at the chamber of commerce. If you don't want to drive the route, take the trolley (25¢ each time you get on) that leaves from the city hall and post office complex on U.S. Highway 321, and hop off wherever you like along the way.

TOP SECRET

Many of the artists living in the Great Smoky Arts and Crafts Community welcome visitors to watch them work. If you're interested in learning more about weaving, glass blowing, woodworking, clock making, or dozens of other disciplines, call the owner of the appropriate business in the community, and he or she will probably be more than willing to set up an appointment to show his or her craft.

91 Roadside Attraction

Back in the days when Dinah Shore encouraged everyone to "See the U.S.A. in your Chevrolet," motor inns were the place to stay. Postwar tourists bought big boats of cars, piled the kids and dogs into the back, and set off in search of America. At night they steered the station wagon into a clean, quiet motor inn and parked right in front of their door. The kids met other kids at the motor inn's playground and pool, and everyone exchanged friendly hellos at the ice machine or pay phone.

Nowadays most motor inns pale in comparison to their multistoried motel and hotel neighbors. Some are home to scruffy year-round tenants; others look as if they're in dire need of either a good paint job or complete demolition. Every once in a while, however, you come across a motor inn that takes you back to a simpler, safer time, a time your own kids never got to see. Our favorite nostalgic place to stay is on the outskirts of Maggie Valley, North Carolina—the Rocky Waters Motel.

Rocky Waters is set back from the road over a narrow one-lane bridge. Lovingly manicured bushes line the driveway and encircle the meticulously maintained heated pool with diving board. The thirty rooms are spacious and clean, although the decor does scream southern wholesale rather than *Southern Living*. There are a standard-issue desk, table and chairs, two comfy queen beds (in rooms with two beds), and a ceramic-tile shower. Only the new cable TV with remote belies the fifties feel.

Tom and Lois Stratton are on-site owners of the Rocky Waters, and they're proud that their simple motel built in the fifties has not had to change much since its expansion in the sixties to compete with the fancier full-service motels and hotels. "We get a lot of repeat business because this is what people are looking for when they come to the mountains," Lois says. "This is a quiet place that is close to everything except the noise."

There *is* noise at Rocky Waters, but it's the natural, babbling kind. The stream that runs next to the motel rushes over a rocky creekbed. Cook out next to the stream on one of the brick grills housed under a wooden shelter, equipped also with a sink, running water, and a picnic table. For the kids and other explorers, there are a few shady "hideouts" on the shore ideal for a game of hide and seek or pirates.

Function reigns over fanciness at Rocky Waters. You can even walk next door to the ski lift that takes tourists up the mountain to Ghost Town in the Sky, Maggie Valley's signature amusement park. Forgo the fast pace for a day. The world will wait and the memories are worth it.

Secret Information

Location: West end of Maggie Valley, North Carolina.
Address: 1510 Soco Road (U.S. Highway 19), Maggie Valley, North Carolina 28751.
Phone: (704) 926-1585.
Rates: Singles $25 to $55; doubles $35 to $75; cabins (2) $85.
Season: Open year-round. Rates are highest in the summer.
Credit cards: MasterCard, Visa.

TOP SECRET

Request a creekside room at the Rocky Waters Motel. These newer rooms have a sliding glass and wooden screen door combination, which leads onto a communal covered cement porch overlooking the creek. You can't help but sleep soundly with the mountain air and the sound of the stream filtering through the locked screen door at night. If you want to splurge, go for one of the two shady cabins, which are just up the creek from the creekside rooms. Both have covered front porches with rocking chairs and small kitchenettes.

92

Yum Jock

So we're sitting in Chef Jock's Tastebuds Cafe when suddenly we hear singing coming from the kitchen—a deep but ragged baritone emanating from none other than Chef Jock himself. The thirty-something, barrel-chested Italian from Ohio is clearly enjoying himself doing what he loves best: cooking. He started making meals for his family at age five and got his first job as a chef at age fourteen. The joy he gets from food not only occasionally fills the restaurant with his voice but also comes through every one of the gourmet meals he serves in his unassuming restaurant just outside Pigeon Forge, Tennessee.

Chef Jock is Giacomo LaJoi, who looks like he should be hanging out on a street corner in Philly rather than sautéing shrimp in the Smokies. He ended up in Tennessee after taking several vacations in the area and noticing that there was a paucity of places to eat much beyond barbecue and fried catfish. He bought a small white building that looks more like a big shack than a fancy restaurant and hung out his shingle. Since then Chef Jock's has become a favorite of locals, drawing upscale customers from Knoxville and beyond.

The atmosphere is, shall we be generous and say, charming. The interior is a hodgepodge of white-painted paneling, ceiling fans, industrial carpet, linoleum, and white Christmas lights stapled to the walls. There are only thirteen tables. The seats are a mixture of patio furniture and torn vinyl and metal chairs. Empty wine bottles line the window-sills, and one wall is covered with photos of the eclectic mix of folks who've dined at the cafe—singer Lee Greenwood, actor LeVar Burton, Tennessee senator Bill Frist, U.S. attorney general Janet Reno, Elvis impersonator Lou Vuto, and David Letterman's mother, to name a few. Things are completely casual: Wearing a burgundy "Chef Jock's Tastebuds Cafe: A True Eating Experience" T-shirt, LaJoi frequently emerges from the tiny kitchen and chats with customers to make sure

The ambiance at Chef Jock's is casual, but the clientele have been a veritable Who's Who.

they are enjoying their meals. He likes to add small special touches to keep everyone happy. When we ate there with one of our daughters, much to her delight he arranged the fruit on her plate into a clown face.

The downscale decor doesn't seem to bother diners, who come for the food. Chef Jock prepares 85 percent of the meals himself, and everything is made completely from scratch. Herbs and some of the other ingredients are even grown in the garden out front. Regularly available specialties include veal Chef Jock (a cutlet sautéed in butter, shallots, garlic, mushrooms, parsley, wine, and cream), and, on the lighter side, angel hair pasta tossed with snap peas and mushrooms and cooked in olive oil, butter, garlic, and basil. LaJoi loves to get adventurous with daily specials. On any given day you might be offered ostrich, venison, frog legs, buffalo, wild boar, or alligator tail (served around the time the University of Tennessee football team plays the Florida Gators). The priciest regular entree is $16.95 and most meals are around $12, much less than you'd pay for similar quality at a big-city gourmet restaurant. For dessert choose a tasty napoleon or a cannoli.

Secret Information

Location: On U.S. Highway 321, just southeast of Pigeon Forge, Tennessee.

Address: Wears Valley Road, Pigeon Forge, Tennessee 37868.

Phone: (423) 428-9781.

Hours: Lunch: 11:00 A.M. to 2:00 P.M., Tuesday through Friday; Dinner: 5:00 P.M. to 10:00 P.M., Tuesday through Saturday.

Reservations: Recommended.

Prices: Lunch entrees range from $4.95 to $6.95; dinner entrees are $10.95 and up.

Credit cards: American Express, Discover, MasterCard, Visa.

Details: Dress is casual. Children are welcome, although there's no children's menu, and finicky kids might have trouble finding something on the menu that they're willing to try (if that happens, just ask for some pasta with butter or marinara sauce).

TOP SECRET

Every entree we've tried at Chef Jock's Tastebuds Cafe is delicious, but two of our menu favorites are appetizers—tortellini (pasta wrapped around cheese and served smothered in marinara or cream sauce) and shrimp scampi (three huge shrimp sautéed in butter, olive oil, garlic, and parsley). We like to order them together as an entree.

School's In

93

The Smokies are stuffed with fascinating places, plants, animals, activities, and adventures never experienced by the average camper. Wouldn't it be nice if you could get an expert in the area to take you on a personal natural history tour to view the wildflowers, insects, birds, and mammals of the park? How about spending a day learning to fly-fish or taking a guided hike from Clingmans Dome, the highest point in the park, to Andrews Bald? Or if you are a budding bird watcher, how would you like to take a basic ornithology workshop that teaches you how to scan the skies for everything from egrets to eagles? Yes, yes, and yes.

All this and much more are available from the Smoky Mountain Field School, a joint venture between the Great Smoky Mountains National Park and the University of Tennessee. Established in 1978, the organization offers the widest and most affordable array of area workshops, hikes, and adventures. Popular with locals but relatively unknown to tourists, the nonprofit program's primary goals are educational, not commercial, and all activities are led by experts such as university professors. While the programs are serious and try to teach you something, they do so in ways that emphasize hands-on learning and fun.

"Taking these courses offers opportunities to learn the secrets of the Smokies from behind the scenes," says Karen Ballantine, a park ranger who serves as the field school liaison between the national park and UT. "The instructors have researched their material for years, and participants are exposed to a high level of expertise."

The school offers a full menu of one-day- to one-week-long programs, starting in mid-March and continuing through November. Many are linked to the season—like wildflower workshops in the spring and foliage forays in the fall. Many activities take place in and around the park, although some are held as far away as the Big South Fork Recreation area on the Tennessee–Kentucky border.

For serious hikers, there are overnight expeditions, like a seven-day, fifty-mile trek from Wayah Gap, Georgia, to Fontana Dam (Secret 12), along the Appalachian Trail. The artistically inclined can choose sessions that focus on sketching, writing about, or photographing Smokies scenery. And those more interested in local history can choose from such courses as "Getting to Know the Cherokees," which introduces participants to the games, language, and philosophy of the Smokies' first residents, or "Mountain Life at Little Greenbrier," which takes participants back to what it was like to live in an Appalachian community a century ago.

Secret Information

Location: Most classes are held in the Great Smoky Mountains National Park, but some are conducted elsewhere in East Tennessee.

Address: University of Tennessee Community Programs, 600 Henley Street, Suite 105, Knoxville, Tennessee 37996.

Phone: (423) 974-0150.

E-mail: fieldschool@gateway.ce.utk.edu.

Web site: www.ce.utk.edu/Smoky/.

Prices: Programs range from $18 ($12 for children) to $325 per person.

Details: Registration starts in February. Programs fill up fast, so plan ahead.

TOP SECRET

The primary focus of the Smoky Mountain Field School has been adults, but more and more family- and kid-oriented classes are being added every year. "Secret Places and Treasured Songs of the Smokies," for example, takes children on a nature walk along the Schoolhouse Gap Trail and teaches them traditional folk songs. If your kids are like ours, though, we bet they'll also like the class called "Amphibians and Reptiles of the Smokies," during which young and old alike get to wade in streams and turn over rocks in search of salamanders, newts, frogs, turtles, lizards, and snakes.

Lost Highway

94

Stand at the barber pole outside the one-chair Riverside Barbershop in Bryson City, North Carolina, and ask a few of the locals how to get to Lakeview Drive. You'll get blank stares. Ask these same folks how to get to the Road to Nowhere and they'll gladly point the way. "Just follow this road here up yonder, past the high school, and you're there."

The Road to Nowhere is actually a bit of a misnomer. Although the road stops abruptly several hundred yards in front of a Tunnel to Nowhere, it carries travelers through one of the most scenic sections of the Great Smoky Mountains National Park. The drive offers fabulous views of Fontana Lake, several little-traveled hiking trails, and regular sightings of deer and wild turkeys (one nonchalantly strolled in front of our car). Don't tell the folks over on the Tennessee side, but the vistas off the Road to Nowhere are some of the most pristine and picturesque in the park.

How this road got started and stopped is a story that stretches back more than forty years. It's all tangled up with the Tennessee Valley Authority and the U.S. Department of the Interior and Swain County, North Carolina. To make a complicated tale short and sweet, the county wanted to build a new highway to help bring visitors to Fontana Lake, and the government offered to construct a compromise route that would stretch from Bryson City across the Smokies to Townsend, Tennessee. Neither road got built, due to environmental concerns and side issues like access to family cemeteries. What remains of the aborted road project, however, offers near-instant access to otherwise remote areas of the park.

The road begins approximately three miles from the Bryson City courthouse square. About .2 mile up it, pull over and enjoy the sweeping view at the North Shore Overlook. Down below is Fontana Lake and to the south and southwest are the Cowee and Nantahala

It's so dark inside the Tunnel to Nowhere that it's almost impossible to see a hand right in front of your face.

mountain ranges. If you're looking for a place to hike, drive (or walk) to the five-mile marker at Noland Creek, park in the lot before the bridge, and hike down the trail that runs from the roadway down to a jeep trail that follows the creek. A one-mile walk south on the trail brings you to the lake. On busy summer weekends you'll share the trail with joggers, trail bikers, other hikers, and even some horse-back riders.

After you've explored Noland Creek, which was named for Andrew Noland, the earliest white settler in the area, move on up another .7 mile to the park service gate. Park off to the right of the gate and stroll up several hundred yards to the tunnel. Walking through the tunnel alone has an *X-Files* feel to it. It's dark and musty and the walls are covered with graffiti. Stop when you reach the middle: It's so dark you can barely see your hand in front of your face. Walk on (if you dare) and emerge in the wilderness. The trail that leads out of the tunnel takes you down to Forney Creek and beyond to some of the most remote areas in the park. If you're a bit less adventurous, climb up to the left on top of the tunnel and savor the scenery before heading back down the Road to Nowhere to somewhere.

Secret Information

Location: North of downtown Bryson City, North Carolina.

TOP SECRET

There's a fairly new trail on the Road to Nowhere called Lake Shore, which leads down from near where the road stops, and that itself was supposed to be a road around Fontana Lake's north shore. A huge acidic anakeesta rock formation, which if broken by road construction would have led to the destruction of the area's stream life, stopped the project. Fortunately, it has left the means to enjoy the beauty of the clear deep black lake that's fed by mountain streams. Park in the area in front of the tunnel and cross the street to find the trailhead.

95

Genuine Pleasure

Walking inside Mast General Store in Waynesville, North Carolina, is like stepping into an L. L. Bean catalog. The main shopping floor is filled with brightly colored Woolrich and Pendleton sweaters, flannels, corduroys, and turtlenecks all displayed on antique dressers and shelves or hung in dark wooden armoires. Downstairs is a hard-core hiker's dream featuring every outdoor item imaginable, from hiking boots to walking sticks to sleeping bags to tents. The only thing missing from the L. L. Bean pages is a few golden retrievers, but you can buy a toy stuffed one in the upstairs mezzanine, along with household items and local taste treats like Mast General Store brand Vidalia onion salad dressing, barbecue sauce, and green tomato relish.

The Waynesville store isn't the original Mast emporium, which is on the National Register of Historic Places (that's way up the Blue Ridge Parkway in Valle Crucis), but it is the closest emporium to the Great Smoky Mountains National Park, and it's historic in its own right. The store is housed in a funky 1930s building with creaky oak floors and a white pressed-tin ceiling, which originally was home to an upscale clothing establishment called the Toggery. The pulley system they used then to relay messages from the main floor to the front office is gone, but the flavor and feel of decades past remains. Just inside the front door, customers sit in high-backed Amish rockers and warm themselves in front of the potbellied stove in winter or cool off in summer under the ceiling fans. Behind the rockers is a dusty glass-front display case featuring century-old merchandise like Grandfather's pine tar soap, liniment, and hand salve.

If you want to truly experience the flavor of the past, walk to the middle of the store to the old Coca-Cola coolers. For eighty cents you can buy an ice-cold bottle of Coke. Pony up two more dimes to taste the pride of tiny Bleinheim, South Carolina—Blenheim's "ole-timey" hot ginger ale.

The inside of Mast General Store is like an L. L. Bean catalog come to life.

Secret Information

Directions: Downtown Waynesville, North Carolina.
Address: 148 North Main Street, Waynesville, North Carolina 28786.
Phone: (704) 452-2101.
Hours: 10:00 A.M. to 6:00 P.M., Monday through Saturday; 1:00 P.M. to 6:00 P.M., Sunday.
Credit Cards: MasterCard, Visa.

Just down the brick sidewalk from the Mast General Store is the Open Air Market, where you can stop under the awning and pick up a copy of Waynesville's own *Enterprise Mountaineer*, or the *Miami Herald*, the *New York Times*, or dozens of other dailies from across the region and the nation. Take your paper with you next door to Smith Drug Store. Built in 1925, it isn't much to look at, but way in back is the old soda fountain that has been transformed by Steve and Melinda Pumphrey into a fabulous breakfast and lunch cafe called Picnic Pleasantries. Snag an umbrella table on the mountain-view deck before you order or sit at the counter or in one of the four and a half booths. The place is jumping at lunch but most of the orders are to go, hand-delivered to downtown workers and the Haywood County courthouse crowd. They know a good thing when they taste it.

Cosby Nature Trail

You Can See the Forest for the Trees

96

The Smokies are filled with sights, sounds, smells, and textures to stimulate your senses, but most people don't take the time to really notice them. The details of daily existence amid the trees often get lost in the sweep of the forest. While a panoramic view of the peaks of the Smokies is breathtaking, no less dramatic is what you find when you take the time to focus on smaller slices of nature.

The perfect place to do that—especially with children—is the Cosby Nature Trail on the northeastern border of the Great Smoky Mountains National Park in Tennessee. To get the most out of the easy one-mile loop at the Cosby Campground, pick up the self-guided tour brochure published by the Great Smoky Mountains Natural History Association and available at the trailhead. The material is designed to make the trail more than just a walk in the woods. It's a trek that will open all your senses except taste (no munching on the greenery) to the small wonders that most tourists miss.

The trail starts along a roadbed high above a stream. Start matching up the eleven brochure entries to the eleven wooden markers on the trail. First, you're asked to notice the sound of the water and how it changes as you progress along the trail. Some slow spots in the creek almost put you to sleep as you step, others pulse with water, and you subconsciously pick up the pace. Next, you're focused on the surrounding shade and how it's life-giving to some plants like ferns and mosses and lethal to others that love sunlight. The brochure encourages you to "scoop up a pinch of forest litter and soil, and smell it." Its scent is rich and moist. Then you're directed to find a hemlock needle, crush it between your fingers, and identify a surprisingly familiar smell, one advertised frequently on TV. (You've got to find out for yourself what it is.) Look closely and you'll see brilliantly colored yellow and orange mushrooms, a dam built by beavers, trees marred by the work of woodpeckers searching for a feast of insects, and tree stumps transformed into homes by spiders, beetles, and nightcrawlers.

As you continue to walk through the forest, you'll become aware of layers and patterns of vegetation, the varied shapes of trees and their leaves, and even the different textures of rocks. That's when you begin to see nature as a work of art.

Secret Information

Location: At the Cosby Campground, near the northeast corner of the Great Smoky Mountains National Park in Tennessee.
Season: Open all year.
Details: This is an especially good trail for younger children.

For more information, call the Great Smoky Mountains National Park at (423) 436-1200.

TOP SECRET

The Cosby Nature Trail is a great way to commune with the wilderness for a couple hours, but to develop a real relationship with Mother Nature, spend a night or two at a campground in the Great Smoky Mountains National Park. During the tourist season, however, many of the campsites are fully reserved and those that are first-come, first-served fill up fast. But the Cosby Campground always seems to have space available and is among the most beautiful in the park. Head there, and even when the other campgrounds are full, you're likely to find a place to pitch your tent or park your RV.

Virtual Vacation Planning

97

On a Smokies vacation you can escape modern life and experience the peace and tranquillity of a wilderness that hasn't changed much in millions of years. But a great way to get there is to travel the high-tech information highway called the Internet. There are scores of sources of information about the mountains on the World Wide Web, everything from sites on Appalachian history and heritage to ads for bed-and-breakfasts. Here's a sampling:

• Great Smoky Mountains Park Homepage (www.nps.gov/grsm/homepage.htm). This is the Great Smoky Mountains National Park's official virtual visitors center, part of the National Park Service's ParkNet (www.nps.gov). It has information on the park's history and mission, a message from the park superintendent, descriptions of the park's popular attractions, and schedules of ranger-led programs and special events.

• American Park Network/Great Smoky Mountains National Park (www.americanparknetwork.com/parkinfo/sm/index.html). Operated by the Meredith Corporation, which publishes visitor guides for parks across the country, the Smokies site on the American Parks Network (www.americanparknetwork.com) is an excellent and attractive overview of the national park and environs, with information about activities, history, flora, fauna, and more.

• GoSmokies! (www.gosmokies.com). This *Knoxville-News Sentinel* site features a wide range of articles by the newspaper's staff on places to go and things to do in the area. Features include the Hike of the Month and columns by Carson Brewer, one of the best local chroniclers of mountain life.

• Gatlinburg Visitors and Convention Center (www.gatlinburg.com), Pigeon Forge Department of Tourism (www.pigeon-forge.tn.us); Bryson City homepage (www.greatsmokies.com); and Cherokee Indian Reservation homepage (www.cherokee-nc.com).

Operated by various tourism promotion organizations, these sites offer a broad but buyer-beware assortment of ads and public relations information on places to stay and eat and things to do at the big-four gateway towns to the mountains.

Secret Information

Several of the places mentioned in this book have electronic mail addresses or World Wide Web sites. References to Internet addresses are included in each of the following secrets: the Blue Mountain Mist Country Inn (Secret 65), Cataloochee Ski Area (Secret 82), *Christy* (Secret 16), Elderhostels (Secret 66), English Mountain Llama Treks (Secret 99), Forbidden Caverns (Secret 35), the Great Smoky Mountains Railway (Secret 29), Hickory Haven (Secret 86), Jubilee Community Arts at Laurel Theater (Secret 73), Kids Camps in the Smokies (Secret 33), Mountain Harbor Inn (Secret 81), Mountain Laurel Chalets (Secret 43), Nantahala Outdoor Center (Secret 44), Rafting the Big Pigeon River (Secret 63), the Richmont Inn (Secret 100), Smoky Mountain Field School (Secret 93), Smoky Mountains Kudzu (Secret 87), Twin Valley Bed and Breakfast and Horse Ranch (Secret 61), and the Von Bryan Inn (Secret 32).

TOP SECRET

Visit the 100 Secrets World Wide Web site at www.100Secrets.com, or e-mail us at Smokies@100Secrets.com. Tell us how you liked this book and pass along any secrets you've uncovered on your Smoky Mountains vacation.

Ye Olde Steakhouse

Where's the Beef?

98

We have a confession to make. Although most of the time we try to eat right—salads without dressing, steamed veggies, grilled skinless chicken breasts, and other low-fat foods—we sometimes get a craving we just can't ignore. We want a steak—a big, juicy, bad-for-your-belly, horrible-for-your-heart piece of pure beef. We try to ignore the yearning and munch on a couple of rice cakes, but eventually it's too much to take, and we have to hop in the car and head for Ye Olde Steakhouse in south Knoxville, Tennessee. Call us recovering carnivores.

Unlike all those chains that want you to think they're serving beef straight from Texas or Australia, the log-cabin-style building on Chapman Highway (Secret 22) south of Knoxville is a true steakhouse. Open the door and you're suddenly hit with a blast of greasy smoke from the flames that shoot up into the air from the grill at the end of the main dining room. There cooks who have been working at the restaurant for as long as twenty-seven years expertly grill to perfection slabs of meat as large as thirty ounces. The place is loud with the chatter of people having a good time. It has a definitely kicked-back country feel, with almost every inch of the walls of its four dining rooms covered with mounted fish, mountain antiques, University of Tennessee sports memorabilia, a yellow jacket's nest, a wagon wheel, an oxen yoke, and family pictures from owner Helen King.

"It's just real homey," King says. "People sit and look, then they get up and walk around to see what they can see." Even the chairs hold small surprises: The backs of many are inscribed in Magic Marker with words of wisdom, such as "Brevity is the soul of wit."

King and her husband, Bunt, opened the place in 1968. He died in 1987, and she now runs it with her three children. "My main job is to give hugs," she says. Customers come back again and again, and she

Open the door to Ye Olde Steakhouse and brace for the blast of greasy grill smoke that will tease your tastebuds. (Photo by Liz Duckett)

seems to know them all. "See the lady in the blue dress?" she'll say, pointing to a diner across the room, then adding wickedly, "She orders two pieces of key lime pie to go every time she's in here, and she takes them home and eats them herself."

The menu is full of what we call Big Food. Red-meat selections include T-bone steaks, filet mignon, and prime rib. The $32.50, thirty-ounce "sirloin for two" is enough to have leftovers to take home. For those who aren't caught in the grip of a beef craving, they serve such items as shrimp, swordfish, stuffed flounder, and chicken. Each table is also set with a plastic crock of soft cheese, which is impossible to resist spreading on a selection of crackers. There are seventeen different kinds of homemade desserts; our recommendation is the Hershey Bar cake. Come hungry.

Besides consuming mass quantities of fatty food, you'll also risk your health by breathing. There's no nonsmoking section, and the mix of cooking food and cigarette smoke can sometimes get a bit thick. King has installed what she calls an "ozone machine" to clear the air, but it seems to do only a middling job. Still, if we were worried about our health, we'd never eat there.

Secret Information

Location: On Chapman Highway in Knoxville, Tennessee.
Address: 6838 Chapman Highway, Knoxville, Tennessee 37920.
Phone: (423) 577-9328.
Hours: 4:30 P.M. to 9:30 P.M., Sunday through Thursday; 4:30 P.M. to 10:30 P.M., Friday and Saturday.
Prices: Entrees range from $8.95 to $32.50; children's dinners are $4.95.
Credit cards: American Express, Discover, MasterCard, Visa.
Details: Beer is served; bring your own wine or liquor. Need we add that dress is casual?

TOP SECRET

Ye Olde Steakhouse is situated on a curve on a busy thoroughfare and is easy to miss, even though it's only fifteen feet from the road. Look for the billboards and keep an eye peeled. Coming from Knoxville, it's five miles from the Henley Street Bridge over the Tennessee River. For those coming from Gatlinburg and Pigeon Forge, take U.S. Highway 441; from the junction with Tennessee Highway 66 in Sevierville, the restaurant is about twenty-five miles north on the right. There are a few parking spaces in front of the old log building, but most are in the back. Ye Olde Steakhouse is most crowded on University of Tennessee football game days, when the wait can last up to two and a half hours. Drop by, however, and you might just catch some coaches or players dropping in to celebrate a victory or mourn a loss.

99

I Remember Llama

For all of his adult life, Bob McIntyre has been an avid hiker and backpacker. A few years ago, though, he severely hurt his knee and feared that his days exploring the wild were behind him. But rather than give up the life he loved, he and his equally adventurous wife, Cathi, decided to take a couple of llamas along on their wilderness treks to do their backpacking for them. They fell in love with the friendly, sure-footed charmers. The couple eventually founded English Mountain Llama Treks, which offers guided backcountry trips through the mountains without requiring guests to carry their own gear. The McIntyres have a stable of about twenty-six llamas, from babies to fully grown animals, on their fifteen-acre farm in the English Mountain area in Tennessee north of the Great Smoky Mountains National Park.

Llamas, which are distantly related to the camel and prized for their wool, are perfect hiking companions. They have centuries-old training as beasts of burden in places like the South American Andes. They create minimal impact on the land as they graze, and each can carry from 50 to 120 pounds of gear. Better yet, they're friendly and gentle. "Most llamas enjoy going out," Bob observes, "and they seem to love little kids."

The McIntyres lead llama trips through the magnificent Pisgah National Forest, which is on the border of Tennessee and North Carolina. Journeys range in length from seven hours to four days. Bob and Cathi personally lead each trip and there is no regular schedule; guest demand determines when they go camping and for how long. The llamas carry tents, sleeping bags, coolers, roll-up stools and tables, guests' personal gear, and fresh food—not the freeze-dried variety common on most wilderness outings. "After a meal we all waddle down the trail because we've eaten so much," Bob says. Being freed of the burden of carrying backpacks allows guests to

English Mountain Llama Treks co-founder Bob McIntyre leads llamas E. T., Beasley, Biltmore, and Rocket Man on a jaunt over the Max Patch loop trail in Pisgah National Forest.

focus on natural wonders in the Pisgah, like the 2,350-acre Max Patch natural bald, a vast treeless open area of heath or grass at 4,650 feet at the top of the mountain.

Most clients Bob and Cathi host are not experienced campers or backpackers, so each trip is geared to the abilities of the least-experienced member. Trekkers, however, should be in good health and able to cover four to six miles a day at a moderate to leisurely pace and up to eight miles in an emergency. Children are welcome as long as they can handle the hike; llamas can't be ridden if a kid gets tired. Llama trekkers have ranged from an eight-year-old boy to a seventy-seven-year-old grandmother.

Secret Information

Location:	Off Tennessee Highway 32, south of Newport, Tennessee.
Address:	738 English Mountain Road, Newport, Tennessee 37821.
Phone:	(423) 623-5274.
E-mail:	McIntyre@hikinginthesmokies.com.
Web site:	www.hikinginthesmokies.com.
Prices (per person):	Day trek with lunch, $60; two-day, one-night trek, $180; three-day, two-night trek, $270.
Reservations:	Required.
Credit cards:	None.

TOP SECRET

Take a hike leading a llama and you might want to have one of your own. English Mountain Llama Treks has the coy creatures for sale starting at $750. Be warned, however, they need a lot of space, food, time, and attention—and the neighbors might wonder where you got that big goofy-looking dog.

Rich History

100

Although the Richmont Inn was just built in 1991, every corner of it reeks of history. The upscale bed-and-breakfast tucked in Laurel Valley in Townsend, Tennessee, is a carefully crafted tribute to the culture of the Smokies. "We wanted to honor the little people who were big in heart," owner Jim Hind says, "the people who made major contributions to the mountains but who are relatively unknown in history."

Hind and his wife, Susan, spent two years researching Appalachian legend and lore before opening the Richmont. They constructed the inn to look like a classic cantilevered barn—a design imported to East Tennessee from Europe, in which the second story overhangs the first. The historical architecture, however, is the only thing barnlike about the Richmont. Inside, it's an elegant blend of eighteenth-century antiques, French paintings, and chic country charm. The intimate dining area faces huge windows that look out on Dry Valley (so called because the stream runs underground) and Rich Mountain. In the mornings, guests savor the view while they down full breakfasts of French-baked eggs and rich bacon (baked with herbs, flour, and brown sugar). In the evening everyone gathers amid soft music and candlelight for superb desserts like the inn's signature Crème Brulée Kahlúa, which has won *Gourmet* magazine's Grand Prize Award.

Each of the ten guest rooms pays homage to a different character in Smokies' history and is decorated with antiques from the period in which that person lived. The Horace Kephart Room, for example, which honors one of the first journalists to write about the area, is dressed up like a mountain lodge and features 100-year-old barn-wood paneling. The entire upper floor of the inn is dedicated to Native Americans like Chief Sequoyah, who invented the Cherokee alphabet. All rooms are air conditioned and have private baths, fireplaces, whirlpools for two, king-size beds, and balconies. The inn recently added an

The Richmont Inn has been constructed to resemble a classic cantilevered barn, with the second story overhanging the first.
(Photo courtesy of Richmont Inn)

Appalachian-style outbuilding trimmed with 150-year-old barn wood, where guests can gather to watch TV, exercise, or play games. A greenhouse in which the Hinds nurture the native wildflowers, shrubs, and other plants they use for landscaping is also open for exploration.

Spending a night or more at the Richmont makes for not only a romantic and luxurious getaway but also a wonderful history lesson taught by people with a passion for the uniqueness of their home.

Secret Information

Location: Laurel Valley in Townsend, Tennessee.
Address: 220 Winterberry Lane, Townsend, Tennessee 37882.
Phone: (423) 448-6751.
Fax: (423) 448-6480.
E-mail: richmontinn@worldnet.att.com.
Rates: $95 to $145.
Credit cards: None.

TOP SECRET

Owners Jim and Susan Hind organize special events at the Richmont Inn throughout the year. Most Saturday nights feature performances and lectures by local musicians, storytellers, naturalists, and others. Dulcimer player Bill Taylor, for example, might drop by to play "Amazing Grace" and other traditional tunes, or Fred Alsop, author of *Birds of the Smokies*, might talk about the best places to bird watch. Call for a copy of the inn's newsletter, which lists upcoming activities.

Send us your secrets

Did you discover a great lesser-known place to stay, eat, shop, or have fun during your vacation in the Smoky Mountains area? Drop us a card or e-mail with information about it. If we include your suggestion in a future edition of *100 Secrets of Smokies*, we'll pay you fifty dollars.

Okay, here's the fine print:
- If more than one reader submits the same secret, the one who sent it in first will get the cash.
- Please include your name, address, and phone number in all correspondence.
- Rights to all submissions immediately become the property of Media Development Group, Inc. Sorry, we cannot return submissions.
- Media Development Group, Inc. reserves the sole right to determine whether to pay for a submission. This includes cases in which a reader submits a secret that we have already learned about from another source.
- By submitting a secret, you agree to the above terms.

Send your secrets to:

100 Secrets of the Smokies
P.O. Box 6672
Oak Ridge, Tennessee 37831
E-mail: Smokies@100Secrets.com
Web site: www.100Secrets.com

INDEX